COMMON SENSE
SUPPLY
MANAGEMENT

TALES FROM THE
SUPPLY CHAIN TRENCHES

DR. TOM DEPAOLI

INTRODUCTION

Common Sense Supply Management is dedicated to all the people that I have worked with and for in my career. This book is a summary of many of the lessons that I learned in my supply management and management career. I have used a very different approach in this book than in my original publication, *Common Sense Purchasing*: I am using a storytelling technique. I have included and updated some of the best excerpts from my previous book.

I have discussed many of the real life events or stories that occurred in my supply management career. The stories are told as they happened without any distracting notes. I do hope that the reader will gain valuable insights from the stories. In order to protect some clients and colleagues, I had to keep the stories somewhat less detailed than I would like. I have added much on process improvement, Lean, and Lean Six Sigma.

The book does somewhat serve as a desktop guide to supply management, but it can't meet every need of every reader. Most of my experience has been with large and medium-sized corporations. However, the principles do apply to small businesses.

I sometimes repeat what I consider important points about principles for the reader. Be patient with this approach it works. The journey of supply management, although sometimes tedious and frustrating, was great fun for me. I hope that the reader enjoys the journey as much as I did.

CONTENTS

CHAPTER 1:
TALES FROM SUPPLY CHAIN MANAGEMENT TRENCHES

In this book, I've decided to use a different approach to sharing my supply management knowledge with readers. I believe people learn more from stories and a real life events than from a textbook. The following stories are meant to get you to think about improving your supply management strategy. Some of the stories are good management lessons. In some of these tales, I was very fortuitous (lucky); others were the result of having talented people work for me and teamwork, and still others were the result of just hard work and massive amounts of homework. I do hope that you, the reader, enjoy the stories and learn from them.

Mega-Negotiations Story

A supply management colleague and I had been working diligently for a year to try to standardize MRO (Maintenance Repair and Operating) parts to include pumps, pipes-valves, electrical, and operating supplies. We divided the storeroom parts into these four bucket areas. These were storeroom-related parts for a multi-national chemical company. We used a market-basket sourcing approach. We had conducted numerous strategic sourcing cross-functional teams and had worked hard to get our engineers to select standardized parts for our plants. These sessions were long and arduous. We had reduced the number of suppliers or OEMs (Original Equipment Manufacturers) in many categories to one or two. Our goal was to gradually replace the existing parts as they wore out with the new OEMs and strive for standardization in the MRO arena. We had a systematic, well thought-out plan for doing this, and had negotiated contracts with the OEMs and distributors. We were approximately 80-percent complete, which was quite an accomplishment for the fifty North American plants.

Then the company suddenly announced that they were in the initial stages of planning a $5-billion expansion in the United States. The winning five plants had already been selected. Some of them would be entirely new plants, and the others would involve major rebuilds. The capital expansion was to start in six months. We were faced with managing a major capital expansion and a significant spend in the MRO area. We met with the vice president of engineering and decided to have a strategy session with him and the five selected plant engineers. We decided to have a one-shot bidding meeting with our preferred suppliers in Louisiana. We had a very good idea about the dollar amount of spending in the various buckets for the expansion. The capital job estimates had already been made and approved. We had four bucket areas in MRO: mechanical, electrical, pipes-valves, and operating supplies. We already had cost-plus pricing contracts for 80-percent of our MRO. We did, however, still have at least two preferred suppliers in almost every major component MRO area, such as pumps.

I suggested that we leverage the hard work that we had already accomplished. We would announce the capital expansion at a preferred-supplier meeting and give an approximate future-dollar spend in each of the four buckets (areas). We obviously had considerable leverage, and many of the bucket dollar numbers were huge. We had fairly accurate data from recent expansions and the capital-job estimates. We then established these ground rules for the bidding process:

1. There would be only one round of bids. We urged the suppliers to give the bid their best shot. We didn't have the time to manage multiple bids.

2. We announced that we would, in many cases, narrow down the areas where we had two preferred suppliers to one, unless we had a good business reason for keeping two.

3. Although we'd negotiated some significant total-cost-of-ownership savings in the current contracts, we were open to enhancements from the suppliers and distributors.

4. We told the suppliers that we would not accept their standard spare parts packages as we had in the past. We would challenge their typical spares packages, but would be especially open to creative ways of them controlling and managing the spares at minimal or no cost to us.

5. OEMs could work with distributors to propose any additional creative services to provide us.

Quite frankly, we had no idea how this mega-negotiations process would work. Fortunately, we had done a lot of supplier consolidation before this process. We had not even predicted cost savings or eventual outcomes—we just did it. As the bids rolled back in, it was obvious that our suppliers had done their homework. All told, the cost and other savings amounted to 20 percent of the $5 billion. We were stunned. For the next year, my supply management colleague and I had to endure "Here come the billion-dollar boys," whenever we entered a meeting.

Yes we were good and worked hard, but we were also very lucky. The fact that the company was spending that much capital at one time when we were transforming to supply management really helped our leverage.

Mega Change: or, Getting Everyone Out of the Comfort Zone (Including Me)

One particularly difficult transformation process was my third—which meant that I should have learned many lessons already! Nonetheless, only two people in a department of twenty showed any enthusiasm for supply management transformation. Most of the personnel had long-established relationships with suppliers, and the department was divided into subgroups identified by the materials or services that they purchased. Thus, people were so-called "experts" in their particular material or service. Unfortunately, many pursued their own materials and services without regard to the impact on the total product or machine.

I first moved the entire department to a new area in the company. I changed everyone's title. I developed a glossary of supply chain management terminology that they were to use in all their correspondence. I challenged them to prove to me that they were not only getting the best price for their particular materials, but also the best total cost of ownership. I also made them create or refine metrics to measure their suppliers' performances. I expected strong data to prove it. I insisted on monthly written reports from everyone. I gave them a template for the report, and they had to adhere to it. I insisted that they evaluated their savings in terms of the market for their materials. Thus they had to learn the market well for their particular materials. If the market price had gone down by 5 percent for the year, and they only saved 2 percent that was not good performance. For the first month, just about everyone was in an uproar just trying to cope with all the changes. This was beneficial; they had less time to resist the changes.

Finally I started to broaden their knowledge of our final product. The engineering department and I conducted training classes on the packaging machine that we sold. The engineers educated us on the particular sections of the equipment and their functions. Although they were experts in a particular material, I reminded them, our paying customers wanted to dialogue with us about the machine they had purchased, not just a particular material. We all had to become better at understanding total-machine functions and technology. The purpose was to make them realize the possible impact of some of their material change decisions on the function of the machine. I wanted to transform them into machine-function experts—not just particular-material experts.

This tactic paid off. Our salesmen and engineers became more comfortable with my department members and invited them into meetings with our paying customers. They directly interacted with the customers and could understand their needs and concerns. When serious issues developed, we brought in our preferred suppliers to help in the problem-solving sessions.

I also insisted that our people accompany our field reps periodically on service calls to get a better feel for what they had to go through with a customer while servicing the machine. Their feeton-the-floor time in a third-world country, working side-by-side with a service rep, gave them an enlightened perspective of the challenges we faced with our worldwide customers.

Amazingly we all survived this massive change, and we gained enormous respect with our colleagues in the company. Customers would call customer service and then ask to talk to some of my supply management people about issues.

Mini-Storerooms: Or, Moving The Storerooms To The Customers

One of the first supply chain projects that we did at a large chemical company in Alabama which involved frequently used MRO parts by the maintenance folks. Highly paid maintenance personnel ($30 per hour) were driving in pickup trucks, in pairs, to go to a central storeroom to pick up basic and frequently-used parts. The time lost was enormous. We were a chemical company, and our expertise or core competency was not in storeroom- or MRO-parts management. We started a supplier search for distributors with expertise in management parts and storerooms. We decided to basically outsource the management of these frequently used parts to the distributor. They examined our storeroom data, provided us software, and soon discovered the one hundred parts most-frequently used by our maintenance folks.

They then set up many free-issue or mini-storerooms throughout the large chemical plant's grounds. Our maintenance folks traveled or walked to these areas to get the parts they needed. The distributor maintained and restocked the areas. The distances were much shorter and conveniently decentralized. The maintenance people set up a steering committee with the distributor to review parts usage and add or subtract parts to the mini-storerooms. The process was greatly simplified, and the maintenance people soon developed a high degree of confidence in the distributor and the streamlined system. Then the distributor offered to reorganize our storeroom and barcode all the parts at no charge. We quickly agreed.

In another month, a shocking development occurred. Many of our maintenance people had no confidence in our current storeroom system. We publicized a return-any extra-parts-with-no-questions-asked week. This was run much like a fine-free day at your local library. Our maintenance people returned over $2 million-worth of bogey or just-in-case inventory that they had been squirreling away in their toolboxes and other areas. They'd done this because they'd had zero confidence in the old system. Our new supplier accepted the parts back and gave us a large credit for the returned parts that were still usable. The distributor kept us abreast of any new storeroom-management techniques and technologies, including the RFID (Radio Frequency Identification Device). We developed a long and lasting relationship with them which became the model for our other chemical plants.

From An Infinite Number Of One-Off Machines To Five Models—Just Like The Auto Industry

I once was the purchasing manager for an equipment manufacturer that sold high speed paper packaging equipment all over the world. Each machine that was ordered could have as many as 200–300 options on the machine. It was absolute chaos in purchasing and in plant assembly. Engineering change authorizations were routinely lost or not updated. Our salesmen were paid a commission on each machine sale, and the more options that they could convince the customer to purchase, the more money they received. Customer service had a difficult task keeping track of exactly what options each customer had on its machine. In summary, each machine was one-off, or unique.

We were at the end of our rope in purchasing and could not keep up with the specifics of each unique machine order. Our suppliers in many instances could only plan one machine at a time. We took the initiative to sit down with engineering and try to understand the 200–300 machine options. I came up with the approach of trying to use the automotive-industry's options model. When you order a car, you usually order option packages. These packages have a group of options in each package group. If you order automatic transmission, you also get cruise control whether you want it or not. The upper-end option package usually has everything in it. Obviously, the higher or more elaborate the package that you order, the more expensive the price of the car.

We decided on five option groups or levels for our machines. The salesmen at first balked at the idea until we convinced them of the overall benefits to the company. Various machine options were grouped together in ways that made sense for the customer, and the higher the option package, the more costly the machine. We would not allow our customers to select between 200–300 options anymore. Our customers had to decide which level of machine they wanted. Each level featured a certain group of options. However, the options made sense and complemented each other. We thus narrowed down the choice to five different styles of machines, rather than a nearly unlimited number. The impact on the entire supply chain and internal efficiency was enormous. Our suppliers could plan their production better, and our assembly department no longer had to constantly deal with as many engineering changes.

These changes had not come a moment too soon for us. The next year, we increased our sales by an astounding 500 percent. We had outstanding orders for 111 machines. The simplification of models enabled us to avoid a single late delivery. We did not have to add any additional personnel in purchasing.

Customer-Service Tactics: Why Getting In The Field Works

I once headed a walk-in customer-service center at a large US Navy base in Virginia. Often when customers arrived at the center, they were in various states of panic, looking for parts that they needed immediately either because of a breakdown or because their ship was about to go to sea. I always did my best to get them the parts that they needed and to make sure that these parts arrived at their ship or place of work. Often I just gave the parts to them to hand-carry back to the ship. Sometimes, unfortunately, I could do nothing to help them.

After one hectic weekend filled with nonstop crises, I sat down with my entire customer service crew and brainstormed how to prevent such chaos and last-minute parts pleading. We came up with an aggressive tactic to try to prevent these last-minute emergencies. I set up a schedule where we would go out on the piers and visit ships, introduce ourselves, and go over their requirements with them before they were to go to sea. I spent at least two days a week on the pier visiting the ships and talking to the ships' supply officers. We all got plenty of exercise walking on the concrete piers. Three of my chief petty officers also conducted these visits. As part of the visit, we asked them to rate us, our service, and to recommend any improvements. Based on their input, we actually adjusted our hours and manning. We constantly sought out our customer's opinions on what additional parts they thought that we ought to be stocking. We also took their orders right on the ship when we were there and delivered the parts the next day.

After about a month of these tactics, we noticed a considerable reduction in the number of walk-ins, and a severe reduction in the crisis visits. We then made our ship-visit program permanent.

If you are a supply management professional, you need to use these same tactics with your customers, both internal and external, in addition to your suppliers. You don't learn much by staying in your own office. We didn't just take customer surveys; we made sure we visited them in person on a frequent basis. Because of this tactic, we greatly reduced many firefighting adventures in supply management. We incorporated suggested administrative changes and streamlined their work processes with them, especially the ones linked to supply management. Many suppliers shared with us what their other customers were doing, and we soon adopted many of their improved processes.

As a warning, this approach requires tremendous discipline— and a schedule that you adhere to with a passion. I do believe that you'll learn more about your customers on his first-hand, systematic basis than with any other approach.

Building Relationships With A Japanese Supplier, Using Baseball As Common Ground

There are also humorous ways to build relationships. When I was in Tokyo, Japan we visited the local sake bars at night, my Japanese colleagues wanted to get to know me and learn more about me personally—not just my credentials. I soon discovered that I did know a lot about a topic that they loved: baseball. The Japanese are enamored with baseball. I got into long discussions about Billy (Martin) Ball, "small ball," Earl Weaver's Three-Run Homer strategy, and various other baseball tactics. Since I had played baseball myself, it was very easy for me to get enthusiastic about it. They hung on every word that I spoke about baseball. I won over the whole team by putting a pillow down on the bar floor and demonstrating how to execute a stand-up slide into second base. I executed it well, even with a little too much sake. I finally won the whole team over when I also showed the team leader how to do it. He executed it perfectly, to the cheers of everyone. The next day, we made great progress on our project, and whenever I tried to explain a difficult point, I used a baseball analogy. It almost always won them over.

How To Get Employees To Trust You

There's no easy way to get employees to trust you. Here are some ways that I've used over the years:

1. Keep your word. One of things that I've always done is made sure that I do what I've told them I was going to do. Nothing impresses employees more than keeping your word.

2. Admit your mistakes. Another good tactic to use is to always admit your mistakes—don't try to cover them up.

3. Train them. Employees appreciate when you invest the time and effort to train them. Make sure you have a training plan for all of your employees.

4.   Behave ethically. Employees expect you to lead by example and to live by your word.

5.   Communicate daily. Use as many different channels of communication as you can. Remember some people have preferred channels for communication.

6.   Get to know them. Take the time to understand what they do and respect what they do.

Let's talk about this last one for a moment. One of the things that I always did was sit down with my employees and not only watch how they did their jobs, but also have them teach me how to do their jobs. Then I would actually perform some of them.

This really grounds you as a boss. You get a good understanding of the aspects of their job and what they go through daily. If I worked for a company that had well-documented work practices, I would read these *before* I sat down with the employee. This gave me a good background to learn more rapidly. It also showed the employee that I was very interested in what they did.

Early in my career, when I was a team manager of a national brand startup project, I was there when all the equipment was installed. We had to make sure that the equipment was centerlined, and we also had to run it ourselves. Often on the third shift, when I saw that an employee was tired, I would go up to them and tell them to take a break in the lunchroom, and I would run the equipment myself for ten or fifteen minutes. I also participated in the standard operating procedure for the machines and the safety rules. I also made it a point to play cards with members of my crew on breaks. I usually won at sheepshead and euchre.

Helping employees when they have a personal problem is often never forgotten. I once had an employee who had to be the caretaker for her mother. She would often have to take hours off to deal with this issue. I would go into her office and try to do as much work for her as I could, including dealing with people who needed her help. When she finally had to take family leave for a couple of weeks, I did my very best to do as much of the work that she normally did as possible. She had dreaded the prospect of coming back and seeing all the work that had piled up, and she was in disbelief when she returned and saw that I had taken care of much of the work.

She said to me, "I've been here for twenty years, and no one has done anything like that for me." After this, I could not have a more loyal employee, and she often volunteered to take on the most difficult assignments.

Customer-Centric Organization Tale

I once was involved with a major transformation of a worldwide logistics organization. At the start of the transformation, they had twenty-six divisions. They had decided to reorganize and needed some basis for the reorganization. I suggested that we first do a marketing plan, which was greeted by disbelief and catcalls. I basically explained my strategy and said that first we had to find out what our market segments were and agree on that. We did fifty focus groups, deep marketing research and narrowed down our customer segments to six.

After presenting the marketing plan and getting agreement that the six segments were, in fact, our customer groups, I recommended that we organize around these six market segments.

The buzzword at the time was customer-centric organization. However, all we wanted to do initially was look at gaining efficiencies among the twenty-six divisions.

What we did next was look at all twenty-six divisions and determine exactly what each did. We then looked at it in terms of which of the six customer segments they served the best, or were most likely to serve the best. Much to our surprise, there were no "in-between" divisions; each division fell within a particular customer segment. All of the division heads agreed with their customer segment alignment.

Once we presented this information to the CEO, he immediately suggested that we consolidate twenty-six divisions into six. Each division would have a customer champion, whose main mission was to meet the needs of that particular customer segment. After much work, job analysis, and feedback from the division heads, we consolidated into six divisions. We eliminated over 600 positions, but we did avoid layoffs with attrition and by offering early retirement.

The thing that I failed to mention about the story is that this organization was also a supply chain management organization. Over the years, they had gotten out of touch with their mission and customer base. Once the reorganization was executed, when we got our customer-service metrics, we were pleasantly surprised to see that they'd improved dramatically. Now the organization's employees could focus more on customers and their needs, instead of defending their silos. Soon other organizations asked how we had accomplished this, and we shared our data with them.

Benchmarking Via The Shopping-Cart

Many organizations brag about their benchmarking efforts and how good they are at it. I once worked for a large paper company, and a lot of our spending in supply management was for packaging materials involved in the making of toilet tissue and paper towels. I was involved in materials management, plant scheduling, and packaging engineering at the time. Fortunately, all the people involved in these operations reported to me. We were also very fortunate that the plant manager had a materials background and was open to suggestions from us. At first, we went out and tried to get information from various paper institutes, but we found this data to be unwieldy, expensive, and not up-to-date.

Then we just decided to use the shopping cart. We went out to various supermarkets and stores and purchased as many of our competitor's products as we could. We basically dissected them and the materials that they used, looking to see what they had done differently than we had. They were using cheaper materials but had suffered no disconcerting quality drops. Over the years, we had not kept up with the advances in materials. In addition, the process to get new materials approved was unwieldy and required corporate approval. This discouraged almost all the plants from taking risks in the materials area.

We put a matrix together of us versus all the competitors and all the materials. We also showed the estimated cost differential and savings on a one-year basis if we in fact adapted the most cost-effective material of our competitors. We couldn't believe the numbers, and we were shaking when we presented the matrix to our plant manager. Lucky for us, he brought it up at a staff meeting, and told all the department heads that they were to cooperate with our materials trials and experiments. He also told us to not ask permission from corporate for the trials and to just do them; if any flak developed, he would run air cover for us.

I was fortunate to have an extremely enthusiastic people working for me. In addition, we got superb cooperation from our shop-floor staff. People are competitive, and when they heard that our competitors had made it work, their personal pride took over, and they wanted to make it work. It helped when we showed them the competitor's product and the materials that they were using. Then they knew that this was not just us making up a plan and trying to achieve some impossible goals.

We assembled a trial plan, started intense packaging-supplier visits, took shop-floor people along with us to talk with our suppliers, and asked further advice on changing over to the new materials. Our suppliers were extremely cooperative in making suggestions. Many of them were in the plant on the shop floor when we ran the trials. They could see firsthand any issues we had, and they made suggestions on how we could improve the tests. We were stunned at how rapid and successful the trials were.

Many of the materials specifications had been in force for years and had not been updated, challenged, or changed. Let me give you an example—one that will make you shake your head. Many of our corrugated boxes for toilet tissue products were placed in two-, three-, or four-color cases. Our marketing people had free reign to decide how many colors they wanted on their cases. All of the cases had barcodes on them, and when they went by our production counter reader, the reader counted them as one case.

Obviously, it's vitally important to have an accurate production count. Unfortunately, the *red* barcodes were extremely difficult for the reader to read, and often they were skipped or sent to an off-count conveyor. Bottom line, it hurt our production-count accuracy.

The only person who usually even saw the case that our product was in was the stocker in the store—not our final customers. The cases were usually cut up, bundled, and recycled. Our plant manager soon convinced marketing that a one-color black case would be the cheaper, more efficient strategy. We were very lucky to have a plant manager who understood materials, and as they say, "When your man is in the White House, pass as many laws favorable to you as you can."

In the first year, we saved over $20 million.

Have Your People Attend Production Meetings— It Works

One of the first things that I had my supply management people do was attend the daily production meetings that took place in the plant. I required them to attend the meetings, which were often conducted early and before staff personnel normally arrived in the plant. When I had attended production meetings, I heard various staff functions being criticized by production personnel. My logic to my people was that if they are going to bad-mouth you, you should be present to hear it and defend yourself, or take action to correct what they're complaining about. What soon happened was that the production people quickly realized that informing supply management people of potential problems gave us a much better chance of helping them with spare parts or maintenance orders. It also eliminated any of the normal message handoff noise that accompanied many of their requests, and demonstrated that we had an urgent desire to help solve their problems. We also brought in supplier experts to help with technical problems and issues that arose. Soon my people were accepted as contributing members of the production teams.

Office Supplies Dense-Pack Sourcing

Once I was tasked with completing an office-supplies sourcing search for a client in a major western state city at their headquarters, which housed approximately five thousand employers downtown. I had experience completing four other such strategic sources of office supplies, so I had a fairly good idea of the competency of the suppliers and their pricing structures. I also knew which additional total-cost-of-ownership practices to ask for, such as desktop delivery, consolidated billing, and electronic catalogues. It was an ideal situation for a supplier, because it was one delivery spot for significant sales volume. Composing the request for a quote was straightforward, and I used many of the requirements that I had previously used in requests. My client was eager to get the sourcing process underway and completed quickly.

However, I soon discovered that there were three other large companies in the same block housing an additional fifteen thousand employees. I saw an opportunity to pool our volumes and presented a proposal to my client. I had shared our expected price reduction and other savings with them prior to the engagement. Now I proposed to the client to construct a request for quote for all of us for office supplies, thus providing more leverage. I named it the "dense-pack" approach because, once again, the winning supplier would have concentrated deliveries in a close area, which would significantly reduce the winning supplier's transportation costs. The purchasing managers were skeptical at first, but luckily none of the other companies were direct competitors.

The hardest part of this approach was next: convincing the other three companies of the merits of this approach. Fortunately, all of them were familiar with supply management and strategic sourcing. I had to show the expected savings and get them to agree to the total-cost-of-ownership reduction items. Gathering the usage data was another challenge, but we believed that we had fairly accurate volume data when we went out with the request for a quote. Getting agreement to go with the winning quote was not as difficult as I had anticipated, and all four companies had two representatives on the sourcing team.

The results were fairly astounding, and we doubled the expected price savings. The winning supplier then offered a cafeteria menu of total-cost-of-ownership savings and enhancements that each customer could select.

A Transaction-Based Lean Six Sigma Success

When I took over as head of a procurement division for an integrated paper company, there were three plants with over $500 million in purchases per year. I was to transform Purchasing into Supply Management with some Lean Six Sigma tools. Plant senior management decided to downsize my department at the plant where I was located from eight to four, starting from day one. The plant manager was not committed to the transformation attempt and wanted it to fail. I decided to do everything in my power to disappoint him.

At the first meeting I had with the department team, two people started to cry. They didn't know how they were going to keep up with the work. I pledged that within six months, they would have so much spare time; they would be coming to me, asking me what to do to move the business ahead. They all laughed at the statement.

I volunteered to take over buying of one of the major components in the plant. Of course, I had no idea about the workload involved in the buying process. The next day, four file drawers of paperwork for the component were moved into my office. I spent a week creating a database to help me manage the component, which had no previous reliable information. Eventually a supplier helped me improve the database and ordering process.

I soon found out that purchasing data was scarce or nonexistent. Purchasing employees could not give me any good summary statistics and were so caught up in firefighting that confusion reigned supreme. No one could adequately explain the purchase-order process. There were no standard operating procedures. Undaunted, I rolled up my sleeves and typed purchase orders myself just to get an idea of what happened. We did a process map of the purchase-order process. We locked the doors to the department while we had process-mapping meetings.

We all went on a data expedition, and since I knew some computer programming and could query from the company databases, we started to compile our data. We discovered that we had approximately forty thousand transactions or buys per year. By using a Pareto chart, we saw that over 80 percent of the purchase orders were under $200. The majority of our purchases were small-dollar items. Additionally, only twenty people made about 90 percent of these buys. They were our *superusers* or *power requisitioners*. We decided to concentrate on them and educate them about our efforts to transform the entire process. We designed a short-order purchase form for purchases under $1,000 that they could use. They participated in the design of the form. No interface with purchasing was required for the form. The middleman (purchasing) was eliminated. The only catch was they had to buy from a list of our preferred suppliers. If they wanted to deviate from the list, they needed to get our approval.

We did a new process map for the short-order form with the superusers participating. We created a manual and SOP for the superusers that included the preferred-supplier list, contact information, and basic purchasing terms and rules. We posted a process-flow map in the department for everyone to see.

Our workload was drastically reduced, and the buyers didn't have to worry about these small purchase orders. In addition our suppliers remarked that the error rate on these short orders was greatly reduced. We recognized superusers who had error-free months, and who worked well with suppliers. We eventually switched to purchase cards for these twenty superusers, which practically eliminated all paperwork.

Finally we had time for supplier rationalization or reduction-and-strategic initiatives. Again, we mined the data and found out that we had over twenty thousand suppliers. With hard work and consolidation of buys, we got that number down to 209. We set up preferred suppliers and greatly simplified the entire process from requisition to payment. We standardized payment terms, which greatly relieved accounts-payable's workload—and they soon became our allies.

In four months (not six), my employees had the confidence and trust in me to come to my office and admit that they had nothing to do that day and asked what could they work on to move the business ahead. Most of this progress was due to using some simple Lean Six Sigma process improvement tools.

Hell Hath No Fury Like A Supplier Scorned

We once had a machine-tool supplier who had lost our bid spread the rumor that the supplier-selection team was not fair in the process and that the supplier that we'd selected was going to go bankrupt. Fortunately, we had the union president and many shop-floor people on the cross-functional selection team. They were irate, and they worked hard to convince plant personnel that the process had been fair and held team meetings to show the work that we'd done. The supplier that we'd selected also gave us documents on their credit rating from our local bank. The rumor soon collapsed.

The new supplier provided us a personal computer to directly connect to them and access their inventory. They came onsite and rearranged our inventory, bar-coded it, and purchased back obsolete tools. The shop-floor personnel again surrendered their "bogey" or hidden inventory and developed great confidence in their service.

Often, disgruntled suppliers will sow seeds of doubt—especially when a new supplier is selected. The best advice is to totally ban them from your property, and forbid all further contact with the company. Purchasing should have the first and last say on which suppliers are even allowed on company property. Don't back down on this issue. Backdoor purchasing by other departments, especially engineering, is rampant in many companies. Nip it in the bud. Punish the "Backdoor Bugaloo" dancers.

Using One Bureaucrat Wisely Story

I once had an employee who was at the pinnacle of bureaucratic behavior. She insisted on following procedures and rules to the nth degree. She would correct the grammar and spelling of her colleagues incessantly. She was particularly pedantic with supplier's paperwork and their following of our directions. She loved being a bureaucrat, and just loved bureaucratic procedures. Unfortunately she had little if any skills in relationship building or strategic initiatives. I was faced with the dilemma of what to do with her skills since relationship-building and strategic thinking were becoming requirements in our supply management organization.

To the rescue came ISO 9000! I needed a department ISO 9000 internal auditor. Anyone familiar with this certification realizes that the maintenance of ISO 9000 records and keeping them updated is a severe time-consuming headache. I placed her in charge of the ISO 9000 records and the massive three-ring binders in our department. Since we were transforming so fast, and the procedures were changing so fast, it was difficult to keep up with the changes—but not for my newly appointed internal auditor! When we received our formal periodic six-month outside-auditor reports, our department was always first with the least amount of discrepancies! I reinforced her vigor in this role by having the vice president of supply management visit our plant and give her a recognition award for her diligence. I also gave her a major assignment to research supply management best practices and internal procedures, and then compare them to our current procedures. She diligently completed these comparisons.

Women And Supplier Relationships

Women have, by far, better relationship-building skills than men. This is not meant to stereotype genders—it is just a skill set that most women are a lot better at than most men. Supply management depends on relationship building, especially with suppliers. I took advantage of this many times throughout my supply management career. Whenever I started to have a relationship issue with a supplier, I sent one of my personnel who were the best at fixing it. Most of the times I sent a woman, and she was highly successful.

We had an alliance supplier who was experiencing difficulty in getting accepted at our plant and had not yet built up trust with the plant's customer end-users. The previous supplier liaison in my department had been a man. Although the supplier metrics looked good, this trust issue still could not be resolved. I then assigned a new female supplier liaison—a well-respected supply management professional with over twenty years of experience at the plant. The first thing she did was talk to many of the end-users to try to find out what their issues were with the supplier. What she found out was that the supplier plant representative didn't have very many personal skills and could not engage our shop-floor people in relationship-building conversations, banter, or small talk outside of business. Our end-users wanted more than just technical expertise—they wanted a representative who could relate to their personal needs, and have a sense of humor. At first she went to meetings with the representative and tried to get him to be more open with our plant personnel. Unfortunately, not much progress was made.

She then requested the supplier to assign an alternate representative, and asked the shop-floor personnel to be part of the selection team. They selected a much more personable representative, and the alliance became much stronger.

Never Underestimate Politics And Personal Vendettas

When I was a Six Sigma black belt at a logistics command in the military, we had an administrative process that broke down so many times and took so long that we suddenly received a notice of a Congressional investigation. Our agency head was furious and sent me and another black belt to fix the process immediately. We decided to conduct a kaizen with the process-work team, which knew that it was being scrutinized and had to come up with a fix.

They were very cooperative and very knowledgeable of the work process. We painstakingly went through the entire process map and all the delays. We worked nonstop for three days. We completed all eleven tools for a kaizen and then brainstormed possible solutions. We did significantly reduce the number of steps, handoffs, and process time. We believed we were making progress, and then I started to look more closely at the history and timeline of past completed projects using the old process. One step in the process was having the final recommendations approved by another department before a final decision was made. It was not talked about very much in our meetings. Much to my surprise, this was the biggest bottleneck and took the most time. It was not until we took a lunch break that one of the process workers took me aside and said that their department head and the approving department head, who had to approve the final recommendation, had been at personal war for years. I once again verified that this approval step was in fact the longest process step in the timeline.

We decided to add a formal process step or escalator clause. We mandated that the approving department had forty-eight hours to approve or disapprove the recommendation. If they could not make up their mind, the agency's deputy would then make the decision within the next twenty-four hours. We thus effectively destroyed this logjam.

After six months of gathering data with the new process, the average cycle time went from 179 days to twenty-two days.

Luck Helps, Or My E-Procurement Software Installation Story

I have extensive functional-procurement and supply management experience. This attribute attracted an e-procurement software company to hire me as a sales representative and software installer. I went through a rigorous software boot camp and went to my first installation client. I was obviously very nervous and wanted to make sure that the client was satisfied with my performance and that the software installation went well.

The client was a software company also, but not in supply management. This was the equivalent of installing plumbing in a plumber's house! They were highly critical of the capabilities of our e-procurement software and its limitations. I soon had a long punch list of aspects of our software that they were not satisfied with or wanted improved. Being new to the company, I diligently sent every one of their requests up the chain to corporate development. I also made sure by phone that development completely understood my request.

The night before go-live day, I received the software installation disks from corporate. Much to my surprise, the installation disks were version 6.0, and the client had only paid for version 5.0, I could not get anyone to give me any direction on what to do, and with the deadline fast approaching, I decided to install version 6.0. As I went through the testing, I was relieved that the new software was up and running and stable. It had passed all the benchmark tests. I, however, was not looking forward to the meeting with the client the next day. I was sure that they would find even more issues that they wanted improved.

I started the meeting, and before I could get into the training plan, one of my client's harshest critics spoke up, "Mr. DePaoli, I want to commend you. I signed onto the software very early this morning and checked all the punch list issues that we had talked about, and they were fixed. I apologize for being so critical of you and your company."

Although I was more shocked than he about these circumstances, I remained composed and just replied, "Great! I stayed up all night modifying the software to solve those issues." To my amazement, I said it convincingly and with a straight face.

What had happened was that, like a good soldier, I had sent all these issues to development using the system required, and they had incorporated them directly into version 6.0 as a fix or as an option. Our client was ecstatic, and within three months, the client requested to upgrade to version 7.0. They specifically asked for me to personally install it. Luckily, I was already involved in another major project, and our vice president of sales assigned another installer to them that (he told them) I had recommended for them. They remained loyal customers for many years.

Adversarial Negotiations: Why Beating Suppliers Constantly Doesn't Work

I once worked for a German-owned parts company that only believed in adversarial negotiations. Their idea of being a strong negotiator was to just continue to beat up the other party in the negotiations. Preparation didn't matter. I just needed to be aggressive, and yell and scream a lot. Often we had corporate personnel sit in on the negotiations, and the more that I beat up the other party, the more favorable the report back to head-quarters.

This was, of course, a total cop-out to the supply management transformation process, which values relationship building and cooperation. No matter how hard I tried to convince them of the error and futility of their tactics, they insisted on beating up the other negotiating party. No preparation was really required on my part—just thinking of the theatrics that I'd use.

The other parties were wise to us, however. They knew that they could expect at least three sessions or negotiations beatings, so they never gave us their best deal initially and made us work our theatrics on them at numerous sessions. This was obviously a waste of everyone's time, but the culture of the company was such that this tactic had to be used. If you did not use this tactic, you were viewed as weak and as not getting the best deal for the company.

When I left the company and joined a progressive supply management company that believed in Win-Win negotiations, I remembered the prices of some major items at the previous company that we had negotiated with the same supplier. The new company's prices were at least 20 percent less, with many favorable total-cost-of-ownership aspects.

The lesson is: Constantly beating up your suppliers doesn't work.

Sometimes Your Worst Suppliers Are Your Own People

Once when I was in the paper industry, we were in desperate need of base napkin paper stock to convert into napkins because our own machines had extensive downtime. Our sister plant on the West Coast came to our rescue and shipped us base-paper rolls to meet the need. We were initially glad to get some help. We soon discovered that they had loaded the rolls in boxcars and extensively damaged them. We had to cut off the damaged paper. The boxcars were also loaded in a haphazard manner and took very long periods to unload. On top of these issues, we came to realize that they must have seen this as an opportunity to ship all their old off-quality rolls. The quality was terrible. The rolls took twice as long to convert into napkins. We never asked for their help again. All too often, a company's own internal divisions don't treat their internal customers with any degree of respect. The standards must be at least the same if not better than for your final customer. Supply management should lead the setting of these standards. The lesson here is that even your own internal company suppliers must have standards and metrics to adhere to, or you will be taken advantage of.

Outsourcing Plant Cleaning

I was once given the project of outsourcing the cleaners for three manufacturing plants in Texas. The company had negotiated this outsourcing initiative with the union. Although the company had negotiated this agreement, emotional feelings were still high and bitter. We went through a long and detailed supplier-sourcing process on this. I also knew that many of the people in the plant were not in favor of the outsourcing. We had shop-floor personnel participate and collaborate with us in the selection process. We decided early on that that there would be a quality-assurance committee.

The supplier that we selected had a good track record at similar manufacturing plants. We had done our research well and looked at the supplier measurement systems that the other plants had created. We adopted many of them. We also decided to take a chance. We provided a suggestion box for our employees, where they could either criticize the cleaning done in their areas or make suggestions. One rule that we had was that the supplier had to answer the suggestions within forty-eight hours. We also insisted that the leader of the plant crew had to meet on a regular basis with the plant manager and listen to the plant manager's concerns.

At first, the bogus complaints poured in. The plant-cleaning crew leader decided to meet with the plant manager on a more frequent basis and to take the plant manager out to areas of the plant that were criticized. The plant manager soon discovered that many of the complaints were not as serious as characterized in the suggestion box. The cleaning-crew manager built up a good rapport with the plant managers at the three manufacturing plants, and after about two months, most of the employees had to admit that the cleanliness of the plant had improved dramatically. This one-on-one strategy guaranteed the honesty of the process.

Train the Trainer Works

I worked for a company that had decided to put in a massive, enterprise-resource-planning system. I was in the supply management area and had been assigned to MRO and specifically the storerooms of the company. The ERP or Enterprise Resource Planning software company insisted that they have representatives from each area of the company to help them in the definition phase. Since no one in my area volunteered to work with the software company, my boss appointed me. I first viewed this assignment as another tough task and more work on my already full plate. I went to a rigorous three-week train-the-trainer program that the software company provided. Then I struck out and visited all the storerooms and conducted training sessions for the storeroom personnel.

Unfortunately, many of the personnel didn't really believe that the system was going to come their way, and they didn't pay very much attention to my initial training sessions. They wanted to continue with the old disjointed systems that they used to run the storeroom. The training classes were hard enough, but with apathetic employees, they became difficult and painful. I did, however, pick up expert knowledge about how the storerooms were run, their inventory systems, and their ordering systems.

When the ERP system went live, I was deluged with requests to repeat the training sessions. The employees had come to the realization that they had to learn new systems, and they had to make them work. I literally would fly to six or seven plants in a week and re-conduct the classes. I made sure that I conducted these classes with patience and enthusiasm. My good efforts in these sessions, as reflected in the ratings I received, soon got back not only to the software supplier but also to my boss. Even after these additional training sessions, I acted as an informal help desk to many of the storerooms throughout the country.

Eventually I left this company, and I was hired by a competitor of the ERP software company. I showed them what I had done in the classes that I had conducted and the ratings that I'd received. Fortunately for me, the module that I knew was very similar to theirs.

North, South, East, And West: Dividing Your Storeroom Into Four Quadrants ("Buckets")

We decided to divide up our MRO, or go into four buckets. Buckets is just a way of grouping similar are complimentary parts or products. The buckets were mechanical, electrical, piping and valves, and operating supplies. When we were finished with the sourcing, we had four distributors' suppliers who could handle each of these buckets. We realized that we were not experts in storeroom management; in fact, our storerooms were poorly organized and undermanned. We decided to take a chance and basically divided our storeroom into the four quadrants, with each distributor in charge of the quadrants. What happened next was amazing. Not only was the storeroom much more organized and professional, but they also pooled their talents and made sure that their software directly interfaced with our software. We benefited from their expertise in storeroom management. Every time a new development or technology came about, we could take advantage of it.

In essence, we outsourced our storeroom to these four distributors, but it was on our plant site. We'd never hit our inventory-cycle count goals for as long as I could remember. A month after the four quadrants were organized, we exceeded our goals. Our employees were ecstatic about how organized the storeroom was, and now they had tremendous confidence in one of the most important things: when our inventory said that we had a part, we *did* have it. Employees voluntarily started to return safety or bogie inventory back to the storeroom. Our storeroom employees stepped up their customer service and now delivered many parts directly to the person who wanted it, without the customer even coming into the storeroom. With our suppliers' help, we transformed our storeroom into a modern facility that was a showcase for the rest of the plant.

Why Requiring Employees to Write Monthly Letters Works

Whenever I was involved in transforming a supply management organization, the first thing I did was insist upon monthly letters for my employees. I also insisted on a specific format and encouraged them to incorporate metrics and data into their monthly letters. I wanted them to be focused not only on their personal goals but also on our department goals. Initially, the whining from employees was fierce. These letters formed the basis of my own monthly department letter, and served as an accurate record for my employees when I did their performance reviews.

This type of discipline is essential for the success of supply management. It helps focus your employees on goals, supplier metrics, and planning. I insisted that they always have a section that told me what they were going to do in the upcoming month. This enabled us to have a dialogue on their goals and what they should be doing. I especially encouraged them to give kudos to people who had helped in the supply management arena—especially suppliers.

Requiring your employees to develop the discipline of writing a structured monthly letter won't make you popular—at least not initially. It pays off big time in the long run, and I highly recommend it.

Talent Trumps All

One of the things I've always done in my personal life (Yes, I *have* managed to have one!) *was* coach athletic teams—especially young athletes at all age levels. Nothing makes a coach look more like a genius than talent. This is why when you hire someone in supply management, it's critical that you go after the most-talented people you can get. Certainly the corporate structure and systems can help people succeed, and they play a dramatic role in how successful supply management can be. However, individual talent and drive trumps all. When you have outstanding employees who have ambition to go higher, make sure you give them the tools and training to reach their goal. Take care of your best.

Doing Vulcan Mind Melds With Distributors

One of the things I soon learned about distributors is that they are a great source of information. They have had relationships with suppliers for years, and they can readily and easily tell you which one of their suppliers that they deal with is superior. They also usually have better supplier-tracking systems than many organizations. Having a distributor that you can trust give you feedback on a potential new supplier is a must. Feedback from another organization or competitor is valuable. Distributors have a much broader sample field to compare from and recommend. You must have a very strong and trusting relationship with these distributors in order to take advantage of their expertise in this area. My advice to you is to work on building that trust.

Using Models To Help People Visualize

Empowering employees to make decisions is a powerful advantage for a company and encourages employees to offer good ideas. Employees who work a process every day are usually the most knowledgeable about the work and the processes' inefficiencies.

I was put in charge of a major plant-expansion project, which included developing a master plan and the layout of the new, expanded plant. The plant had been separated by a highway and had received permission from the state to close the highway and construct a building that would connect the distribution area with the production area. The plant manager and I went house-to-house and met with all the neighbors impacted and personally explained the reasons for the project. Some areas of the plant would not change much, but other departments would have to be totally revamped. We were familiar with the principles of material flow and *Lean*, and worked furiously on producing options for the new, expanded plant. We knew that we would be in competition with other plants for capital and wanted to make sure that we developed a good plan and efficient layout.

One of the ideas that I came up with was to use the massive table in our plant conference room and lay out a basic blueprint of the proposed new layout. The table was filled with the blueprint of the proposed new master plan, and we also provided some three-dimensional models to scale, including such things as forklifts and work in process, which enhanced the realism of the layout.

Then we invited natural work teams of employees to come into the conference room, look at the layout, and "play" with it. We listened to their input and concerns as they asked questions about the layout and made sure we answered their concerns. We made numerous modifications to the layout based on their input and invited them back to see the changes that we had made. One change was to make the aisles wider and make sure we had enough turn around area for the huge parent roll lift trucks.

When we put together our final layout and request for capital proposal, although we were very confident in it, we decided to ask for half the capital dollars that we needed and to construct the building in two stages. During the presentation to the executive committee when we were nearly finished, one executive asked to see the final, complete building layout. He was so impressed with the efficiency of the layout that he convinced the board to approve the funding for the entire building. We completed the expansion within a year, and the plant's employees helped cut the ribbon for the grand opening.

Visibility Of Metrics Works

I usually insisted that the supply management metrics were posted and visible to everyone in the department. Any visitors could also see what we were tracking and how we were doing. The conference room where we met also had our metrics visible, and we updated them frequently. Meetings were structured to review the metrics and they allowed us to talk about improving them. Many departments were afraid to post their metrics because they feared that their underperformance (warts) would be attacked. I welcomed any criticism and often met with folks to strategize how to improve the metric performance.

The metrics were also complied and listed as an appendix in our monthly and quarterly letters. Whenever possible we shared relevant data with suppliers and showed them where they stood versus other suppliers. Nobody likes to be in second place, and we soon noted that when problems arose suppliers responded quickly with solutions not excuses.

Treat Mistakes As Gems

I have made nearly every mistake that there is to make in supply management. The key is to learn from them. Once I handed back the winning quote to the *wrong supplier* on a gears bid, and I had to restart the bid process. The second time around, we made sure that we told the suppliers of the error and the reason for the requote. They recommended that in the future, we only bring in the *winning* supplier, and not discuss any details with losing suppliers about why they were not selected. They had seen too many unethical moves on the part of customers trying to reopen the bids and lead suppliers that were "favored" to rebid and thus become winners of the bid. This was a valuable bit of advice, and its benefits have long since made me forget whatever short-term grief my initial gaffe cost me. The lesson is stick to your ethics especially with bids.

The best policy when you make a mistake—whether with an internal supplier or customer—is to admit your mistake and explain what you will do to make sure that it does not happen again.

I had a policy in department meetings of non-attribution of mistakes—meaning that I didn't want people pointing out the mistakes made by others. Instead, I encouraged my employees to admit their own mistakes in department meetings, so that we could all learn from them and make sure that we didn't repeat them. I usually led off this process with My Mistake of the Week. Once employees see that there's nothing to fear from admitting mistakes and learning from them, you will be surprised how the creative juices flow and suggestions are made on how to prevent them from recurring.

Little Things Mean A Lot To People— Find Out What They Are

People really value little things that you can do for them, but often their bosses don't understand what is important to them. I once was in charge of a huge warehouse complex in San Diego for a one-month assignment. It was January, which is the worst weather month in San Diego. None of the warehouses were air-conditioned or heated. The temperature would fall to the low forties or upper thirties in the morning, and many of the forklift drivers were not used to this type of chilly weather. I could obtain some surplus sweaters for all of the forklift drivers to wear. We set them up in one area of the warehouse so that they could be used by employees when they were cold.

I didn't realize how appreciative the employees were of this gesture until three years later, when I returned in the same month for a similar project. I was told to report to the conference room in the warehouse. Much to my shock, every warehouse employee was in the warehouse was wearing one of the sweaters, and they all greeted me with a standing ovation. That year I secured wool watch caps for them.

Parking Is Very Important

On another assignment I had some slack time and was given a project that no one had volunteered to complete or had the time to complete. I was asked to look at the parking lots and parking spaces in a large integrated plant complex. I was told to see if there was any way to improve the number of parking spaces and/or traffic flow. Not knowing a thing about parking spaces or traffic flow didn't deter me.

I soon got a hold of some aerial photos and through pure trial and error, reconfigured many parking lots but kept the traffic flow nearly the same. I presented my plan to the plant manager, who was stunned that I had "created" two hundred more parking spaces. He immediately approved the plan. We reassigned everyone's current parking place (they were reserved) and had a silent auction for all the new spaces, and donated the money to charity. Over one long holiday weekend, the old parking lines were erased and the new parking lines created. The employees were ecstatic. Many had previously had to park in park-for-fee lots outside of the plant complex.

Inventory Story: Stick To Your Ethics

I was once tasked with a project to justify writing off and streamlining inventory for a large company. No matter what method I tried to justify inventory reduction or inventory automation, I soon realized that my savings were insufficient. I presented my findings to the vice president of supply management. He was deeply disappointed at the numbers and expressed concern that I had not presented enough savings to even justify a project. He seemed to be upset and asked a colleague to recalculate the numbers. The colleague did, and he came up with even less savings. Eventually I got a phone call from the vice president, and he basically asked me to fudge the numbers or make them more optimistic. I told him that I could not support this type of approach.

The next budget cycle, I was called into my boss's office. I was informed that I was being downsized. When I asked for an explanation all I got was some vague reference to managing projects and needed cutbacks. In my heart I knew it was because I didn't "play ball" with the vice president's inventory request.

Fortunately, within two weeks I received a better job offer from a major information technology company. Don't ever marginalize your ethics in supply management.

Be Aware Of Politics: A Travel Agency Story

While it's important to never compromise your personal integrity, company politics are a reality, and sometimes you've got to learn to choose your battles. As Otto Von Bismarck put it, "Politics are the art of the *possible.*"

For instance, we once had a CEO who played golf regularly with the president of the travel agency that all the employees in the company used for corporate trips. (The CEO, of course, used the company jet for his own travel—but that's another story.) Knowing a thing or two about human nature, we foresaw that doing a bid process on travel agencies would be a foolish choice, politically speaking. Instead, we put our energies into working with the current travel agency to improve the process and take advantage of certain discounts and fares. So without troubling the CEO's golf game in the least, we still wound up saving the company millions of dollars.

Reduce Transactions: Make Sacred Cows Into Sacred Steaks

I once worked for a company with a seven-part purchase-order form, and every single purchase order had to be approved by the vice president of finance. People were so disheartened by the abysmal speed of the system that maverick ways of purchasing were rampant. We went to a two-part short-order form for everything under $500, and eventually to purchase cards. We eliminated *ten file cabinets* of forms. People soon had confidence in the systems, and they were much more truthful in expressing their needs. The vice president of finance had more time to get IPO funding and improve our financial viability rather than spending his time deciding who should be purchasing pens and pencils.

Aggressively reduce your company's number of transactions. No one will mourn them when they're gone.

IBM Selectric Typewriter Story

I learned at an early stage in my supply management career to always respect hands-on experience. Many old purchasing departments spent much of their time laboring over tedious tasks like typing up purchase orders—usually for the most mundane items or services. They were swamped with transactions and paperwork, which prevented them from performing more strategic work to move their businesses ahead. I literally had to type purchase orders on a typewriter into purchase-order forms, which usually had three or four carbon copies that you had to squeeze into the typewriter carriage. If you made a mistake, it was quite the task to correct it on all the forms. Otherwise, you just had to type over it and hope that it was readable on the other carbon copies. The forms were usually a different color, which signified who was to receive that particular copy in the company mail. In essence, purchasing departments were covered by an avalanche of paperwork in various process stages.

What I did learn from this process was the information required for each transaction or the fields that would be necessary for future e-procurement systems. I also developed a good understanding of the transaction process and distribution of the paperwork. Thus my function-knowledge of purchasing and supply management was strong. This would bode me well in the future when I actually helped install e-procurement systems.

The day that we all received IBM Selectric typewriters, we thought that we had died and gone to heaven. Obviously, we had increased the speed at which we could process purchasing orders, but we still had to understand the purpose and importance of the information. The lesson here is that technology is important, but understanding the process is much more critical.

How To Rationalize Suppliers Easily: Just Set Supplier-Expectations High

One of the easiest ways to reduce the number of suppliers is to show them what your expectations are and insist that they adhere to them. Many suppliers, once they see the breadth of what's expected of them, simply drop out. This isn't to say that they're bad companies—the fact is, you'll be asking them to do some extra work to service your account, and they have their own cost-effectiveness to worry about or perhaps you're not one of their key clients.

I have provided list of supplier expectations that is shown later on in this book. As you know, in supply management, if you don't ask, you don't get.

When In Doubt About Inventory, Zero It Out

One of the challenges that all supply management personnel face is inventory variation. Inventory accuracy is essential to just-in-time and uninterrupted production. When I worked as a production scheduler, I was constantly frustrated by inaccurate inventory reports that caused schedule changes and missed sales opportunities. Then I instructed plant-production personnel to zero out the inventory or run it out. Thus, if I had scheduled a run of five thousand cases of a certain brand, my instructions were to make sure you hit the five thousand cases but run any remaining inventory out to zero. Thus the run might finish up being 5,015 cases, but we now knew for *certain* what the inventory was at the end of the run—zero. We had zeroed it out.

Supplier Summits And Reviews

Suppliers love to tell their stories—especially their success stories with customers. I always made it a policy to have supplier summits where suppliers could go over their metrics and tell their success stories. We spent extensive effort making them feel welcome and making sure that we provided awards for them, especially when they helped us save money. We encouraged the sharing of ideas amongst suppliers and wanted to hear about the latest best practices.

We also provided some fun activities, like trivia games, competitive games like Jeopardy, and team building events where we could relax and build our relationships. These are important to encouraging openness.

Blizzard Story

Once, when I worked in a plant's materials department, a major blizzard struck. Since I lived less than a mile from the plant, I made it into the plant, but I was the only one who had made it from the entire materials department. Shop-floor employees were required to stay in the plant until relieved. Since many employees could not make it in, we had to find some food and nourishment for the marooned employees who were staying to keep the plan running.

I recalled that one of our suppliers had a truck specifically designed for the off-road and remote-logging areas. On a whim, I called them up and asked if they could go to a local restaurant and get some breakfast for the plant. Not only did they volunteer, but also they brought along a few of their employees to help serve the breakfast in our plant cafeteria!

This act immensely built up their reputation in the plant, and we rewarded them with some additional business over the next quarter. It started an open process with them, and they gladly shared their marginal costs with us for the rest of the year. We soon elevated them to a preferred-supplier status and negotiated a long-term, evergreen contract.

Deer Hunting In Wisconsin Story

As plant-production scheduler, I had put into place a cycle-scheduling concept in a plant in Wisconsin. Everyone knows that there are two sacred religions in Wisconsin: deer hunting and the Green Bay Packers. Many of the managers and employees were still reluctant to buy into the cycle-scheduling concept, even though I had run it successfully for six months. I had discovered a way to minimize work-in-process inventory which included large parent rolls and finished-goods inventory, or actual finished cases, at month's end, which is when accounting took inventory and personally counted it. They were amazed at the progress that we had made almost overnight.

Deer-hunting season was rapidly approaching, and just about everyone in the plant had requested the week off. Unfortunately, only the most-senior personnel were allowed off. By conducting many what-if scenarios, I stumbled on a way to manipulate the schedule and work in process to allow four major departments to shut down during deer week and still catch up with the production within a week. I showed the schedule to the plant manager, who quickly agreed to the schedule. He called a meeting of the plant's steering committee and announced that more personnel would be allowed to be off during deer week. Luckily for me, he attributed it to my cycle-scheduling concept.

Word spread around the mill of my achievement, and I was a now a folk hero. Everyone soon accepted the cycle-scheduling concept and I received some delicious fresh venison.

CHAPTER 2:
RELATIONSHIPS

Relationships are Primary

Supply management covers more breadth and depth than any other discipline in an organization. It's the art of building multiple relationships. Although it covers negotiations, transactions, industry knowledge, market knowledge, and technology, it's primarily about building strong relationships and gaining the trust of suppliers, customers, and colleagues.

I'll say it again: relationship building must be the foundation of any supply management strategy. Many cultures in the world spend what seems to us Americans as an inordinate amount of time building relationships before they get to problem solving or execution. Americans are often impatient with this approach, but it's necessary, especially when dealing with other cultures, and a lesson well learned when using supply management techniques.

A supply management professional must be able to build relationships. Supply management departments often spend excessive amounts of money on technical training. This is fruitless unless a strong foundation of relationships is well underway. Relationships can't be faked, legislated, or forced. Supply management professionals must live relationships and commit to them. Integrity in relationships will always carry the day, impress suppliers, scare the competition, and let the supply management professional sleep well at night. Educational credentials certainly look good, and certifications are impressive, but nothing makes a purchasing professional more effective than developing strong relationships and being true to his word. Spending more time on relationships pays off for all participants.

Once a trust is broken, it's nearly impossible to repair it, so don't neglect your relationships or underestimate how critical they are. You won't be able to climb out of the deep pits that you dishonestly dug. Schmoozing with a supplier is easier than digging. On the other hand, honest dealings, over time, build the solid foundation of respect and admiration upon which a supply manager's success depends.

Relationship-Building Credo

The very best way to build relationships is to always do what you say you're going to do, and to always hold yourself accountable for your actions.

This sounds good, but it's not easy. Working together, on problem solving with the suppliers you are trying to build a relationship with, is always a strong way to enhance relationships. Nothing beats sympathy and genuine caring about their struggles and personal fears. People remember when you take the time to personally help them through difficult times, crises, or issues. During a crisis, if you can help a person solve an urgent problem or issue by going the extra mile, you will get their gratitude and long-term trust. Treating others as you want to be treated is the surest way to build relationships. The Golden Rule works. Use it always.

CHAPTER 3:
BEST PRACTICES AND MY ADVICE

Steering Committees

Steering committee or governing councils are essential for any supply management transformation or major initiative. The key is making sure the makeup has a true cross section of the organization and the commitment of upper management. The makeup should include executives and business-unit leaders. Their key responsibility is to make sure the organization buys into the supply management concept. Another duty is to remove barriers within the organization and guarantee compliance with new rules. A critical responsibility is to make quick decisions when required to, especially on controversial initiatives.

I have often seen executives who don't really support supply chain initiatives attempt to slow down or sabotage initiatives. The best way to deal with these folks is via the steering committee.

E-Procurement And Other E-Initiatives

Supply management professionals can't function well if they don't have access to meaningful data. Strong ERP systems and E-procurement software are a definite plus. Access to spending data allows good analysis and triggers more projects and initiatives. Unfortunately, over the course of my career, I have worked with many companies that had poor spend data. This severely threatened to handicap our supply management transformation. Often, I'd contact our key suppliers, who had better spend data than we did. Another desired aspect of spend data is good connectivity capability not only internally, but also globally.

The Supply Management Organization

Nothing provokes as much discussion and disagreement as what is the so-called "best" supply management organization.

Relax. There is no single *optimal* organization. What is essential is that the head of supply management must be at the vice president level. At minimum, purchasing and logistics must be within the confines of the organization chart. The skill sets for folks within the organization include: great people skills, an inclination for strategic thinking, process-improvement skills, and relationship-building skills. Individuals who lack this skill set should not be given high positions in the organization.

What To Do About Total Cost Of Ownership

The concept of *total cost of ownership* (TCO) can be difficult for some clients to grasp. One reason is that deriving this cost requires a good understanding of the internal expenses inherent in a product or service. Unfortunately many organizations don't fully understand their internal costs, an initiative of supply management must be to uncover and expose these costs, especially on key costly materials or services. Standardized training classes should be developed to explain the concept and to help employees discover hidden costs. Obviously when going through the sourcing methodology, total cost must be pinned down.

Process Improvement And Controls

A process-improvement methodology must be established, especially for supply chain processes. The supply management organization needs to adapt Lean, Six Sigma, or Lean Six Sigma. Supply management needs to have certified practitioners in these methodologies. Controls for processes, suppliers, and initiatives need to be in place and closely monitored.

Green Initiatives

Green initiatives are certainly commendable and should be strongly examined by supply management organizations. Customers may in fact demand them from you, so compliance is a good option. It always helps to have green initiatives that save money and waste; here is where Lean can greatly assist you.

Strategic Sourcing

Make sure you have a disciplined collaborative approach to sourcing. Cross functional teams are paramount to get wide buy in to supplier selection. Business units are internal customers and should participate in the selection; however, never lose sight of the needs of what I call the final or paying customer for your end product. Many of the aspects that internal customers feel are important or essential to their efficiency; the external customer has little or no interest in. Never try to short change the external customer.

Supplier Alliances

Always go with fewer meaningful supplier alliances. Trying to manage many so-called alliance relationships is nearly impossible. Pick your alliances carefully. One criterion that I used to select alliance was if the supplier could give us a competitive edge. Another criterion could be a material or service that was a major cost factor for us. It does not make sense of waste time with an alliance with suppliers that provide readily available consumables or other nonessential items. The hard part about alliances is the demand for constant communication and relationship building. Relationships take time and energy. Make sure you agreed to metrics and define clearly your success factors. Always try to select a supplier who has experience with alliances.

Compliance, Risk, And Discipline

Many companies don't keep good track of their contracts and rules of engagement with suppliers. A centralized repository for contracts and agreements is essential. The supply management organization must have a separate department for risk and risk management, especially in the area of backup suppliers. Risk assessments must be done for strategic materials and services and periodically updated. Discipline in buying and compliance to rules has no meaning unless there are consequences for rule breaking. Supply management organizations must enforce the rules and make sure that action is taken quickly when individuals violate the rules.

Inventory

It's essential to work with suppliers and internal customers to reduce inventory levels. Organizations are notoriously lousy inventory managers. Inventory holding costs are always much higher than expected and high inventory causes multiple problems and risk. Each material or service should not have the same inventory strategy. Each deserves a plan based on what the risk is to the organization if an inventory crisis or stock-out occurs. Any initiatives with a supplier that reduces risk should be considered.

CHAPTER 4:
TRANSFORMATION

Here are some suggested steps that you should take to transform your organization into supply management. Transformation in many ways is the new term for reengineering.

Total Spend Assessment Must Be First

Prior to attempting a transformation you need to know where you are spending your money. If you don't, the process is doomed to failure. Here are some questions (checklist) to ask. They work for almost any size company.

- What are your major categories of purchases?

- Are you currently using electronic means for purchasing payment or processes?

- Do you receive summary billing from some suppliers?

- Do you use blanket orders? List them and their annual value.

- Do you have a stores system that is on line and linked to purchasing?

- Does your account payable system link other site systems?

- Do you have releases for some buying?

- How many types of forms of techniques do you use to purchase? List them.

- How many people work in purchasing and accounts payable?

- Do you use corporate purchase cards or online purchasing?

- How many purchasing transactions in a week—month—year?

- What is your dollar volume of purchases in the same above time frames?

- Can you list alphabetically suppliers with basic spend data?

- Can you list stores or stockroom suppliers with the same above data?

- Do you have any special terms or conditions with suppliers? List them.

- What percent of purchase discounts do you capture?

- What are your average days to pay a supplier?

- What is the average dollar value of your purchase orders? How many under $1,000?

- Approximately how many people purchase goods or materials? How many over twenty-five times a year?

- Would you say that your purchases are centralized or decentralized and why?

In a typical company, 75-percent of all invoices are for purchases of under $1,000. At an average cost of $100 to $250 or more just to process the purchase order, pay the invoice, and handle all the related paperwork, this represents a tremendous overhead cost for most businesses. Indeed, in many cases, the cost of handling the paperwork can be greater than the value of the items that were purchased. Many ERP companies offer e-commerce applications that streamline and automate the entire workflow from issuing purchase orders, getting documents approved, paying invoices, and updating appropriate budget and financial systems. These approaches typically result in dropping the cost of fully processing transactions down to perhaps $25, some as low as $3 per transaction — a reduction of as much as 90-percent. In addition the typical analysis reveals that purchasing *spends at least 50-percent or more of their time just on acquisitions or buying stuff!* Don't let the bureaucracy bog down purchasing.

Demolish the Old Culture

The traditional procurement environment dies hard. My advice is to change everything. I call this imposed *mega-change*. Job title, roles, nomenclature even work area change helps. If you are dedicated to cross-functional teams a true purchasing or supply chain professional will be out of the purchasing area most of the time. Not much benefit results from exploring the supply chain takes place at one's own desk. Don't let purchasing folks regress to old habits. It takes a person at least thirty days to gain a new habit. Get everyone completely out of their comfort zone and starting to do the tough work of relationship building.

Best Practices Need A Sanity Check

Know and be an apostle of best practices. Make sure they are sound and have been tested. Focus on your own industries supply management best practices. Always use your gut and experience to sanity check best practices and their applicability to your company. This can't be taught, but it is very necessary. Keep researching best practices and keep them current.

Murphy Will Strike

New systems and new suppliers are certain to *not* be perfect. Make sure you rehearse as much as possible any new systems or procedures. Test and test again. Communicate and make sure feedback sessions are scheduled. Fix it with a sense of urgency. Murphy and his law can be overcome. Be ready to deal with it. Have a problem solving procedure mapped in advance. Follow it.

Get Results Quickly

People and teams need reinforcement. Always go for the simple quick little wins and make sure to publicize the little wins quickly. You will be surprised how little wins can snowball into big wins. Celebrate them. Build that momentum.

Market Your Strategy

Establishing a strong communication plan for your supply management initiatives is critical for its success. Seeking help from trained marketing professionals and communication experts is essential. A continuous communication plan using various media will help overcome the resistance to change. You cannot over communicate. An example of a communications plan I used is listed below:

A Communications Plan:

- Continue to educate top management on the strategic importance of supply management.

- Conduct a surveys of suppliers and publish the results to end-users.

- Conduct an internal customer surveys and act on the concerns.

- Provide continuing advanced supply management education for selected key end-users.

- Conduct quarterly reviews with key suppliers and publish the results.

- Conduct quarterly open supply management forums with a town hall format.

- Publish a supply management newsletter.

- Conduct joint supplier roundtable discussions as required and open to end-users.

- Bring in suppliers to solve design, standardization, and administration problems.

- Update the Supply Management Information Manual as required.

- Publish monthly letters from supply management department.

- Start visible tracking of supply management goals.

- Target selected email news to end-users.

- Create a supply management internal news web site.

- Encourage the formation of a power user news group.

Ask. Ask. Ask Again.

My key rule of negotiations is to ask, ask, and ask. Don't be afraid to ask for anything from a supplier or fellow departments. They can't meet your needs if they don't realize what they are. Asking also flatters them. You will be pleasantly surprised at what you get. Ask.

Terminate The Naysayers

Many supply management folks cannot adapt, and they die hard or resist with a vengeance. Some are recalcitrant kamikazes bent on destroying the new process. There's no easy way to convert them. Start the process to put them on an improvement plan, no matter how painful and time consuming it is. The rest of the folks need to know that you are serious about behavior changes. Stick to your guns. Get human resources help. It's an endurance contest, so don't falter or flinch. They will kick and scream. Like a good parent, you can outlast any employee tantrum.

Follow Through With Mavericks

Shoot a few maverick crows first. When in fact a maverick buy occurs, it can't be ignored. Punishment must be swift, and unfortunately, brutal. Examples are necessary. Don't be shy about being Attila the Hun with maverick buyers. It pays off. The rest of the crows fall in line very quickly.

Once when we just installed a new ERP system, four people in marketing purchased products and services off the ERP system. The CEO insisted that they be fired, and they were. Immediately maverick buys ceased.

Cure The "I Could've Gotten A Better Deal" Psychosis

For some reason, just about everyone not in supply management thinks they are better shoppers or buyers than supply management. They feel that they can always get a better deal. Often, in traditional purchasing, they could, but the additional transaction costs of their maverick deals were killers. Rather than fight them, educate them, and even put the most-vocal, so-called "better shoppers" on cross-functional teams that source suppliers. Use that energy and redirect it.

Pilots Are For Doubters, Naysayers, And Obstructionists

Pilots are good for certain supply management ventures but don't procrastinate or extend them out ad infinitum. It's a good way for the resistance to kill you off. The burden of proof is 51 percent or reasonable. It's not beyond a reasonable doubt or a 12-0 unanimous jury vote. If you use the later criteria you will never have a successful pilot. Make sure one person is accountable for the beachhead and can understand the total picture. Folks love experiments, but remember that the first rule of experiments is to have controls!

People's Roles Must Change

The third "R" in any transformation process is the realignment of roles. Cross-function teams need to be the norm. Supply management personnel will spend more and more time outside of their department or area which is precisely where they belong. Unless the supply management leader is comfortable with this new arrangement the new way of doing business with be severely hampered. Intensive coaching of many simultaneously running teams and tracking their progress will be necessary. Suppliers can also assume some of the role of Research and Development and not think in a vacuum when proposing improvement to materials, parts, or services.

All Non-Value-Adding Work Must Be Skewered

Shed all non-value work quickly. Get rid of it. Don't add any, and don't encourage supply management folks to reinvent any. Don't do any additional work unless it is justified by savings. Don't document for the sake of documentation. Nobody reads it anyway.

Trust Everyone, But Make Sure You Cut The Cards

Trust everyone until they give you reason not to trust them. Cut the cards yourself, however. Be prudent, but not overly concerned with tracking every transaction. Suppliers need to know that you are tracking their performance and that you will take action if they falter.

Make Cross-Functional Teams The Norm

Cross-functional teams work but make sure teams are doing meaningful work. If your supply management professionals are not on cross-functional teams they aren't in the program. Make sure teams have deadlines for results.

Business Process Transformation Will Not Pivot On The "As-Is"

Don't put a lot of faith in the "as is" of business process engineering. You usually won't learn much from your antiquated existing practices. Find out the best practices and strive for them. Dream, do not reminiscence.

Get Supply Management To The Front Lines

Break down your stovepipe and put supply management folks in other departments. Force them to understand other department needs. Let them go to production meetings and participate.

Encourage them to explain to folks what they are doing. Get them on the front lines not the rear bureaucracy. Let them wander about and learn the business. Not much real business knowledge is learned in a cubicle.

Make Materials Experts Into Product Experts, Or, Better Yet, Customer-Needs Experts

The final customer wants the total product to satisfy him. Material experts are valuable, but the customer expects the *total product* to perform. Supply management folks need both the commodity and material expertise and a firm understanding of what the final customer really values in the product. They must become customer centric first.

Build A Supply Management Sandbox

Supply chain folks need their own organization or vice president. They represent almost always more that 50 percent of the cost of goods sold. They are too critical to the success of a company to report to another function. They need to occupy their own sandbox and invite others into the sandbox.

The Change Wave Doesn't Always Hit The Shore

Go with the flow. You can't completely control a major change process. There will be setbacks, and things will have to be revisited. We don't always catch the perfect wave when surfing. When you fall off the board, get back on. Control freaks will not be able to deal with a major change process.

Time Is Moola ($)

Put customers and suppliers first. They will make or break you. Market your plans with a passion, and never compromise your integrity. Don't give up your time unless the benefits are measurable and big. Avoid time sinks. Prioritize relationships, not paperwork. Don't get sucked into endless meetings especially those that don't build relationships.

The Choir Does Not Need A Sermon

Most supply management folks want to do the right thing and be more strategic rather than tactical. Strategy is concerned with long term fixes, innovation and vision. Tactics is usually the day-to-day firefighting. Antiquated processes and systems drag them down and inhibit any creativity. Certainty keeping their morale high during a transformation process is essential. Unmotivated or disgruntled people do not innovate well. Overkilling with strategy, which is borderline ideology, will produce skepticism and distrust. Let them learn and make mistakes that will teach them even more. Make sure they network with each other and share lessons learned. You need to make them grizzled veterans quickly.

Selling Transformation Requires
Saturation Messaging

Your need to spend at least 30–40 percent of your time getting the word out to folks, by many communication channels, on your strategy, messages, and plans. You cannot over communicate, especially about something as radical as transforming the supply chain. Above all, communication requires discipline and a constant reminder, to make sure folks understand why you are using certain steps, programs, and strategies. Keep the metrics right in front of them, and enlist your suppliers to help your spread the message.

Don't Quit

No matter how rough the process gets, losing your temper or wavering from your goals will not help your cause. People can detect the indomitable spirit. You need to make sure that they understand that this is not just another program that will fade away.

Keep telling yourself that you will prevail, and eventually you will!

CHAPTER 5:
LEAN, SIX SIGMA, AND LEAN SIX SIGMA

Demystifying Lean, Six Sigma, And Lean Six Sigma

Lean, Six Sigma, and Lean Six Sigma are just disciplined approaches to problem solving. They are a combination of solution tools used in a systematic manner. Decisions are supposed to be data based. Lean Six Sigma is very disciplined and plodding. All these approaches can be highly successful, but patience and discipline is required.

There's nothing new or creative in the DMAIC process, which is essentially a cookbook approach. Many of the tools used in these approaches have been around for decades, but now they have been cleverly repackaged by consultants. They all require strong top-down commitment and participation, or they will surely fail.

Employees must be strongly motivated to use these problem-solving techniques. From my experience, that only incentive that works for employees is strongly tying in their pay to their participation and results in using these approaches.

The organization where I had the most success with Lean Six Sigma specified that 50 percent of your yearly pay raise was dependent on your commitment to Lean Six Sigma. Very specific metrics were used like becoming a Green Belt, and project success. Many of these initiatives have failed at other companies because top management just gave lip service to their execution. Another aspect that worked for me is that I required vice presidents or above to conduct portions of Lean Six Sigma training classes, and become Green Belts themselves.

These approaches just won't work unless the culture of an organization supports a disciplined problem-solving approach. Most Lean, Six Sigma, and Lean Six Sigma initiatives fail because of the lack of top management support and a culture that does not support their success.

Selecting Projects

Use ROI or return on investment in selecting projects. These process improvement methodologies require a tremendous time commitment from team members. Even for the committed, process improvement is often hard and painful work. Office politics routinely derail or delay projects.

My old rule of thumb on a full-blown Lean Six Sigma project is that it must generate savings of at least $250,000. If it does not meet this approach, consider another, quicker problem-solving method like Lean. If you have no or little data to mine, your project is probably a Lean project, not a Lean Six Sigma, unless you make a major commitment to data gathering first. The danger with this is that you may discover that you are gathering the wrong data, which is self-defeating. The longer it takes you to collect data, the deeper people's resistance to the project will grow. For most projects, the real time limit that people can (barely) tolerate is six months. Anything longer will soon cause revolt. Always try to

Lean a project before you Six Sigma it. Reducing the number of variables and process steps is extremely helpful.

Selecting a Lean Six Sigma Consultant

Experience trumps everything in selecting a Lean Six Sigma consultant. It's critical that the consultant you hire has multiple experiences with multiple projects. Beware of consultants who want to charge exorbitant fees for all the belt classes. You can quickly train your internal folks to become Green Belts, and using the train-the-trainer concept, train future Green Belts.

Certifications are varied and differ from company to company. Insist on references from the consultant and examples of successful projects and tools used in the methodology. There are hundreds of tools that could be used in the process. There are about thirty to forty that are used most frequently.

Consider a fixed hourly rate, but remember that you get what you pay for. Make sure you can retain all the training materials developed during the process. Many of the available training materials are generic, and you will want to retain those customized for your company. Make sure the consultant understands that you want self-sufficiency in two years.

Other Tips On Consultant Selection

The consultants' "people skills" must also be superb. Most members on the problem-solving teams are somewhat hostile to the process until they understand it. Make the contract performance based on the results of the project—not on the amount of training delivered or other parameters. Consider developing online belt courses with your consultant that can be used with great flexibility. Meeting-organization skills and facilitation skills are essential. If you can actually attend a consultant's kaizen event, do. Observing consultants in action is the best way to gauge their effectiveness. Make sure the consultant is a cultural fit for your organization and/or can adapt to the culture.

Some Key Supply chain Metrics for Lean Six Sigma

Here are some key areas that can be examined for potential process improvement methodologies:

1. Inventory cost

2. Obsolete inventory

3. Lead time

4. Backlogs

5. Forecast accuracy

6. Customer service

7. Supply velocity

8. Cost-of-schedule changes

9. Material availability

10. Data accuracy

11. On-time delivery

12. Transaction accuracy

13. Profit/loss margins

14. Returns cost

The point here is that these metrics often have multiple processes that feed into their results, and a Lean, or Six Sigma or Lean Six Sigma analysis could improve them.

Here are some additional areas to apply these methodologies:

1. Contract labor

2. Bids

3. Purchase orders

4. Damaged goods

5. Emergency orders

6. Expediting

7. Backorders

8. Order lead time

9. On time delivery

10. Transactions

11. Premiums or rush-freight costs

12. Returned product

13. Accounts payable

14. Customer service

15. Call centers

Again, the challenge for the supply management professional is picking the appropriate methodology for these issues and areas.

Some Tips for Process-Improvement Meetings

The most common and most egregious mistake that the various process-improvement team leaders make is not having a meeting agenda. The agenda must be published before the meeting and distributed to team members. Team members need to anticipate what to expect in the meeting and what the intended results are—by this, I mean the deliverables. Minutes of each meeting must be taken and published before the next meeting. Minutes must be approved and/or corrected at each subsequent meeting. Always try to have a facilitator and a person taking minutes.

Maximize the visibility in the meeting; make sure all process maps are visible to everyone. Insist that team members get at least introductory training in the methodology. Trying to train team members on process-improvement tools at the same time that you're trying to improve the process is very difficult. If meetings last more than two hours, the leader is not organized, and the members won't be able to function very well.

Always set a goal of finishing at least two deliverables or milestones for each meeting, and push to have them completed. End the meeting with asking the members what went right and what went wrong, and solicit suggestions for improvement.

CHAPTER 6:
COMMON SENSE KAIZENS

Many people get hung up on process and destroy people's enthusiasm for improving the business. There are many simple, straightforward ways to save money and meet customer needs; one tool *definitely* does not fit all.

Some cost-savings projects are simply "no brainers." For instance, simply by switching the default setting on our 1,000-plus printers and copiers to "two-sided printing," we could save our company nearly half of its annual expenditure on paper. Additional savings came from time formerly spent restocking, inventorying, and storing copy paper. No team or process was needed to implement this savings. Encouraging people to think about simple savings like this is the one of the missions of supply management.

A kaizen is a more structured approach, but flexible and quick enough to produce quick results.

Kaizen is a term meaning "continuous improvement." In Lean Six Sigma terms, it refers to a project performed at the workgroup level that will remove waste from a process. These types of projects can be performed quickly (usually in less than two months). I prefer to perform them in two weeks or even less.

I strongly recommend that supply management professionals have at least a Lean Six Sigma Green Belt, so that they can lead kaizens or simple savings projects. The tools of process improvement involved in a kaizen are not very complicated. After conducting many kaizens myself, I have learned some lessons that can make the process more rewarding and efficient.

My Common Sense Supply Management Kaizen Cookbook

This is a discussion of a simplified approach to a kaizen event that I have developed over the years and found to be very successful. I realize that many readers not familiar with a kaizen event or the terminology will have a hard time following this simplified methodology. Please be patient and refer to the glossary at the end of this book for a better understanding of any unclear terms.

Preparation, organization, and visibility are the key success factors for a meaningful kaizen event. The actual kaizen event should be *over*-resourced! By this, I mean there should be many of the elements of a successful meeting. An agenda must be pre-published and strictly followed. There needs to be a kaizen event leader, a facilitator, a timekeeper, and an event minutes-taker or recorder. Any props that enhance visibility of the work must be provided in the event room, including projectors, large flip charts, laptops, or white boards. Everyone in the room needs to be on the same page and seeing the tools being completed. My experience strongly recommends that the event champion participates in the event process and preparation. Discipline is critical. Don't allow any distractions such as smart phones or checking email. Establish strong ground rules for the event from the beginning, and allow no exceptions. Complete all the tools thoroughly, with no shortcuts. Shortcutting compromises the process and always leads to bad implementations. Again, err on the side of *oversourcing* the event.

The team involved in the kaizen event must be the process owners—or, in simple terms, the people who do the work. The more that team members know about the work or the process, the better the chances for kaizen success. I have found, over my years of conducting these events, that outsiders or people who don't understand the work are more of a hindrance than a help. Unfortunately, many times the kaizen event or project champion does not really understand the work process and must be educated before the event commences. The ideal situation is when the kaizen event champions have risen up the ranks in the process area and have done the work themselves.

Kaizen Benefits For Supply Management

The Following Are Benefits
Of Using The Kaizen Approach:

- Rapid improvements, low costs, visible results.

- Process-area experts involved.

- Employs different perspectives.

- Process-owners involved, buy into changes.

- Customer, stakeholder, and supplier participation.

- Improved understanding of organizational processes.

- Learning environment.

- Effective means for changing culture.

Typical Kaizen Results For Supply Management

The Following Are Typical Results That Can Be Expected From A Kaizen:

- Reduced flow or process time.

- Reduced touch time or process steps.

- Increased value-add to the customer.

- Increased quality (percentage complete and accurate, first-pass yield).

- Reduction in work in process.

- Reduced inventory.

- Improved morale.

- Better-educated workforce.

- More projects generated.

- Cycle time speeded up.

Pre-Work Before The Kaizen Is Crucial

Two to four weeks of hard preparation work by the Green Belt or Black Belt and team or kaizen leader is required for a kaizen. The kaizen leader should be a Green Belt or Black Belt. Essentially the first six kaizen tools (there are eleven) are completed or very nearly roughed out before the kaizen event. (See the tools below.) The champion (the sponsor who wants the kaizen done) and kaizen leader must identify necessary subject-matter experts (team members) required for the kaizen. The champion and kaizen leader should author a draft kaizen charter. Hold initial planning meetings with affected stakeholders to communicate the kaizen's schedule, metrics, targets, and Lean tools to be applied. *Most kaizen teams hold three-to-five working meetings before the actual kaizen event.*

Here are some suggested kaizen-event ground rules. The participants of the kaizen should discuss and adopt ground rules that will be in place during the kaizen event and other team meetings. Here are some examples:

- Team is 100% committed.

- No interruptions.

- Stick to an agenda.

- Use of a "Parking Lot".

- An open mind is key to change.

- Positive attitudes are essential.

- Resolve all disagreements.

- No one is to blame.

- Practice mutual trust and respect.

- One person, one vote.

- Everyone is equal; no position or rank.

- No such thing as a dumb question.

Recommended Kaizen Timeline

1. Two to four weeks' hard prep work by the kaizen leader and team members on a one-to-one basis

2. Complete the first six tools before the kaizen event (semi-verify them)

3. Kaizen event (two days to two weeks, depending on the complexity)

4. Implement the kaizen results immediately

Notional Agenda For A Two-Day Kaizen Event

Below is an aggressive kaizen event agenda that should only be attempted when great preparation is achieved and the kaizen event leader is very experienced.

Day 1 Notional Kaizen Event Agenda

The following is a notional listing of tasks to be accomplished during Day One of the kaizen:

- Champion introduction.

- Team introductions, expectations, and ground rules.

- Review of the of charter.

- VOC and SIPOC review and confirm with team.

- Walk the process, gather data and information.

- Optional review spaghetti map or circle diagram.

- Review as-is/current-state process map; confirm accuracy and metrics.

- Identify delays and root out causes ("Five Whys").

- Wrap up and summarize.

Day 2 Kaizen Notional Agenda

The following is a notional listing of tasks to be accomplished during Day Two of the kaizen:

- Review Day One's accomplishments and show Day Two agenda.

- Review delays and causes of as-is.

- Brainstorm fixes to as-is.

- Create to-be process map and get consensus.

- Establish and predict metrics for to-be.

- Create an implementation plan and assign tasks.

- Review results again with kaizen champion.

- Gather all documentation for final report to kaizen office.

Kaizen Tools

I have provided a brief description of the tools used in a kaizen. There are many more books available with more detailed explanations and suggestions on how to successfully pull off the tools. I've presented them below for basic understanding. Most Green Belt qualification courses explain all these tools.

1.0 Kaizen Charter

The champion and the kaizen leader should draft a kaizen charter and show it to all team members and obtain their input. The kaizen leader must identify and invite stakeholders and customers for one-on-one meetings. As with most kaizen tools, a template usually exists for a charter. The more quantifiable the expected gains and current metrics in the charter, the better. The kaizen leaders are to provide just-in-time training to team members as necessary. Refresh participants' training on the tools on the roadmap. Training people on the kaizen tools before the kaizen event is ideal. Trying to combine tool training and solving the problems is often a steep learning curve for many team members. Whenever possible, train first—ahead of the kaizen event.

2.0 VOC Or Voice Of The Customer

There are various ways of finding out the voice of the customers, including interviews, surveys, focus groups and observation. Discover what the customer values most—not the stakeholders. This should drive the efficiency of your process and eliminate non-value adding activities (NVA) (the customer typically doesn't care about NVA activities).

3.0 SIPOC

The kaizen leader will create a Supplier, Input, Process, Output, and Customer (SIPOC) diagram with the assistance of the SMEs to determine the boundaries (fence posts) of the event. The SIPOC is an important tool but can be difficult to execute correctly. This tool usually takes the most time in the kaizen event. Good descriptions of this tool are available in many Lean Six Sigma books.

4.0 Walk The Process

If possible, the kaizen leader and all team members should actually walk the process or simulate it. The purpose is to gather information for the next step, or the as-is, current-state process flow. Often, the process may have to be walked more than once and verified. For a service or transaction process, you'll find that prototypes of the actual forms or emails used in the process make great props!

5.0   As-Is/Current-State Map-Flow Or Value-Stream Analysis

The purpose of this tool is to realistically show the current process to the kaizen team. Various tools can help you accomplish this deliverable, including value-stream analysis, process mapping, flow charts, and swim lanes. The key is to realistically depict the process so the team can understand it and agree that it truly depicts the process no matter what tool you use. The acid test is to show it to people who are not familiar with the process and get them to understand and articulate back the process.

Clearly identify the process-cycle time, delays, handoffs, and any inventories, and try to differentiate between non-value and value-adding steps. Any metrics or data on the process should be summarized and verified. Many of the metrics are geared towards a manufacturing organization and are not very useful to a service organization. This should not discourage the team. The degree and depth of data collection on the as-is/current-state process map is a judgment call by kaizen leader and the project champion. The as-is must be visually presented so that the entire kaizen team can review it and get a consensus on its accuracy.

Don't skip this consensus step. It's painful, but essential.

6.0 Spaghetti Map Or Circle Diagram

These tools are optional but recommended. Their purpose is to show the actual flow or distance traveled of the work or service. The tools can be used to show the flow of people, information, or materials along with handoffs, delays, and queue times. Circle diagrams are very useful for tracking paperwork and approval flows and steps.

Summary Of Tools To Be Completed Before The Kaizen Event Starts

1. Approved kaizen charter

2. Voice of the customer results (VOC) and analysis

3. SIPOC

4. Walk the process results

5. Current state as is process map

6. Spaghetti map or circle diagram.

7.0 Analyze The Delays, Brainstorm The Fixes

Review the as-is/current-state map delays, inventories, and handoffs. Have the team analyze or give the reasons for the delays or the whys, and list them. Talk about root causes if known, and list them right on the as-is process map. There may be multiple ones. If you can categorize them, sort them out. Establish the rules for the brainstorm session and solicit the team's ideas via a brainstorming session on overcoming the delays or fixes. Capture them, and list them right on the as-is process map.

8.0 Create A To-Be State Map

Using the suggested fixes by the team, create the ideal or to-be process map. This often involves crossing out steps, combining steps, and redirection. It gets messy. Clean up the corrections and create a new to-be process map.

9.0 Get Consensus On The To-Be Process Map

Visually show the to-be process and get at least 80-percent consensus on the new to-be process, going over each step. Again, this is a difficult task; usually you'll have some holdouts.

10.0 Predict The To-Be Metrics

Clearly show and try to measure the improvements in the to-be process, to include new cycle time, handoff reduction, inventory reduction, approvals reductions, etc. and establish metrics to measure the to-be. Kaizen improvement goals should be quantifiable, reflect the voice of the customer (requirements), established for both results and change, visually tracked, relevant, measurable, and balanced.

11.0 Create A Kaizen-Implementation Or Project Plan

Create a simple plan to implement all the recommendations of the kaizen, and assign responsibilities and due dates. By all means, do not delay the implementation. The project champion must be in the kaizen's event room and agree to act.

Why Supply Management Must Lead Process Change

No other department in an organization has more dynamic issues to deal with than supply management does. Supply management is continuously challenged by changing global events and demands from both internal and external customers. My advice to supply management professionals is to lead the change and not be a victim of change.

CHAPTER 7:
INFORMATION-BASED NEGOTIATIONS VERSUS WIN-WIN NEGOTIATIONS

Information-Based Negotiations

Information-based negotiations are an approach to negotiations that emphasizes deep knowledge of the supplier and its industry. It varies greatly from some traditional approaches to negotiations. It's not the adversarial Win-Lose negotiation style with the emphasis on game playing, exposing untruths, and taking full advantage of the supplier's weaknesses. This old approach is a competitive winner-takes-all system that rarely builds longstanding, deep relationships with suppliers. Information-based negotiations are not based upon the Win-Win model, either. Information or knowledge is definitely power, but in information-based negotiations, the supply chain professional gains a deep knowledge of the supplier's industry, their margins, and their culture. In essence, this is a deep immersion or empathy with the supplier and their competitive landscape.

Knowledge About An Industry Is Key

In my book, *Common Sense Purchasing*, I state, "The very best piece of negotiations advice I ever received was to know the capabilities of your supplier, their industry, their competitors, their cost drivers, their margins, and their capabilities better than they do! Much easier said than done but it's a powerful tool. It requires a lot of homework, digging, and flat out work. Once a supplier realizes you understand them, it eliminates all the game playing and posturing. You will be surprised how fast they can now focus on real issues and problem solving once they know you can't be bamboozled. You obviously can't do this with every supplier—only the most-important and most-strategic ones. It's a powerful negotiation tactic based on knowledge, not histrionics. Level the playing field with your knowledge! Roll up your sleeves, dig deep, and become an industry expert. Suppliers will be impressed with your knowledge."

There's No Glamour In An Information-Based Approach

The information-based approach requires immense research about the industry, the supplier's financial condition, and competitive forces. Some suppliers may be very reluctant to provide financial information and their margins. The supply chain professional must work to overcome this reluctance and build trust with the supplier. Understanding their culture and their organization is critical. You are, in essence, trying your best to put yourself in their shoes and mimic, as well as possible, their anxieties and fears about the whole process. The information-based approach is not for the fainthearted or for those who do not want to persevere. It should only be exercised for critical materials or services. These are those that have a major impact on your bottom line or can give you a critical competitive advantage. One key guide would be if your customers value the aspect that the supplier brings to the table. Since it requires ongoing market research, and it works better when executives are exchanged (stay in person at the site and become part of the team) however, the resources necessary to pull off such an information-based approach should not be underestimated.

Use The Internet For Your Research

With the Internet, gathering data for the information-based negotiations approach has been made easier. There are numerous industry reports, websites, and search engines that can help the supply chain professional. Nothing, however, beats face-to-face contact and dialogue with numerous suppliers in a particular industry. They all have a fairly keen knowledge of their competitors, which can rapidly improve your overall knowledge. Since many industries are oligarchic in nature, once you understand the top three or four players in the industry, you have a real good foundation from which to open partnerships with your chosen supplier. In addition, ask your fellow supply management colleagues.

Be Systematic

There are plenty of sourcing methodologies available. The important thing is to pick one that is systematic and that you are comfortable with in your quest. Thoroughness is the key in information-based negotiations. In my personal experience with the process, every time that I have skipped a step or not been diligent in my investigations, it has led to the selection of the wrong supplier and major setbacks for the supply chain concept.

After The Supplier Selection, Prepare For Even More Work

After the tough and tedious research, now comes the most crucial phase with the supplier. This is the trust-building phase, with an emphasis on soft skills and mutual learning. One tactic I have used successfully during this initial trust-building phase is to mutually do supply chain mapping of internal processes, but with a twist. The supplier comes to your site and maps your processes, then presents it to a cross-functional team to check understanding. The supply chain professional ventures to the supplier's site and performs a similar mapping. Often, this sparks a new creative exchange of ideas. The information-based approach is continuous, as both parties continue to learn from each other.

Information-Based Negotiations Are The Superior Option

Traditional negotiation styles are short on mutual gain and can't adapt very readily to changing market conditions or competitive situations. The information-based approach has tremendous flexibility to cope with market and industry changes. Information drives decisions—not emotions or one-upmanship. It requires the supply chain professional to become the resident expert on a market or an industry and yields much more significant long-term gains than traditional approaches.

Win-Win Negotiations

Win-Win negotiations have been heralded as a new approach to problem solving, wherein parties strive to achieve mutual gains. The process is very different from traditional adversarial negotiations. The agreement is targeted to be mutually satisfying to the parties. Win-Win tries to separate people and emotions from the problem. Active listening is a must, and both parties try to become problem solvers, use empathy, and avoid blame or judgment. Interests are supposed to define the problem and prod the realization that they are often conflicting. The goal is to be hard on the problems but soft on the people involved. Win-Win encourages the parties to broaden the options. The parties should not judge before mutual agreement is discovered.

Win-Win does have a methodology about options and a process to use to explore and develop options. The key is communicating each other's interests and striving to get agreement in common-interest areas. Constant clarification of these interests, along with honest feedback is essential for the process to work. As with traditional adversarial negotiations, a clear and proper closing is required.

My experience with this process is that it should only be used for critical strategic materials or services because it requires a huge commitment from the negotiating team. I say "team," because the process is not meant for one-on-one negotiations.

As a precursor to this Win-Win method, my *information-based negotiations* would be a great starting point. Gather data to understand the interests of the party that you are negotiating with.

I also find it frustrating that many supply management professionals don't even develop a simple list of expectations that they want from the negotiations before the process occurs. I always have a list of at least three outcomes that I desire from the negotiation session. Leaping into negotiations unprepared is the best way to derail the entire process.

CHAPTER 8:
PLANNING AND STRATEGY

Strategy Trumps Technology

The Institute for Supply Management notes that 95 percent of supply chain departments do not have a procurement strategy or long-term supply management plan. Of the 5 percent that do in fact have a strategy, only half have successfully aligned the strategy with overall business strategy. Don't be afraid to put non-traditional metrics in your plan. Remember, people behave according to the way that they are rewarded. After you have a strategy, you must educate other employees on its tenets and the reason behind it.

Strategy Demands Consistency and Faith

Once you deviate from your strategy or principles, it's difficult to explain this or rationalize it to your skeptics. Don't do it. Stick to your guns and your strategy. The need to classify materials and services into particular categories is essential for the success of supply management. Each material group may require not only a different procurement strategy but also a different acquisition solution. Companies often try to apply the same vanilla acquisition strategy universally to all materials and services. These materials categories demand different strategies, different types of suppliers, and different relationships—along with the use of multiple tools. Currently electronic tools do not exist for certain specific materials needs. They are, however, rapidly evolving. Mobile purchasing is becoming a force to be reckoned with. The placement of certain materials or services into a particular group may vary by company, industry, or a number of factors, depending on the criteria. The key is to have and to articulate a strategy by materials group and to use the appropriate acquisition tool.

Study the matrix below. Don't use the dartboard approach. *Think.* New tools are developing daily.

Some Materials-Grouping Advice

Obviously, you must modify the suggestions below, based on your particular situation:

Leverage Materials

Strategies

- Price leverage.

- Use competitive bids.

- Long-term market agreements.

Possible Tools

- Online auctions.

- Electronic RFQ.

- Hedging.

Strategic Materials

Strategies

- Alliances.

- Long-term relationships.

- Alliance contracts.

Possible tools

- Partnering.

- Collaborative design.

- Software.

- Six Sigma.

- Lean.

Non-Critical Materials (MRO)

Strategies

- Consolidation.

- Improve logistical costs.

- Reduce administrative costs.

Possible Tools

- E-procurement software.

- Exchanges-marketplaces.

- Outsourcing storerooms.

Bottleneck Materials

Strategy

- Minimize risk.

- Replacement or redesign.

- Minimize risk of supply.

Possible Tools

- Value engineering.

- Shared higher inventory.

- Product redesign.

- Collaborative design.

- Six Sigma.

- Lean.

Be Prepared For A Long Struggle

Often in companies and in the traditional culture, supplier relationships have existed for years. The good old boys are really good old boys, and they have cemented their networks. Maverick buying, breaking the rules, and awkward supplier relationships are the norm. Relationships may be strong but are based on the whims or needs of purchasing folks or other internal customers who get their way. Suppliers love a divided corporate house. It's much easier to confuse than impress in this situation. Bottom line, a coordinated and systematic team approach to relationships is necessary. A disciplined strategy that meets the total needs of a corporation and not just a few departments is unfortunately uncommon to many companies. You need a siege mentality, perseverance, and to always being prepared for a long, tough slog. So be ready to constantly be challenged and subject to all types of tricks to derail the strategy. You will either become a keen survivalist, or you will remain a victim. The former is much healthier.

Make Your Followers Out Dream You

Get your folks to out dream you. Get them to state what the purchasing department of the future will look like and dream and build on that dream. When they out dream you, you know you are on the way to purchasing Shangri-La. Visualize future behaviors and performance. Verbalize them. Verbalize world-class behaviors. It helps to ground folks in what you are trying to accomplish. You want them to soar and dream! Let them.

CHAPTER 9:
SUPPLIER TACTICS

Reduce Suppliers First

Radically reducing the number of suppliers is one of the first efforts that must be tackled. You can't have "relationships" with thousands of suppliers. It's difficult enough to have strong relationships with just a few key suppliers. Ruthlessness is necessary. This is not the time for compassion or backing off your supplier-reduction goals. Set the new supplier standards high. You will be surprised. Many will not want to participate under your new, higher expectations. Does the supplier add value, or is the supplier a product of misplaced loyalty? We once cut a base of five thousand suppliers to 252 in three months. It can be done, but ruthlessness was required.

How did we accomplish this monumental task? One simple way was that we sent out correspondence to all the suppliers explaining to them our new supplier expectations. Below are some examples of the expectations that we used. You can adjust them for your needs.

Examples Of Supplier Expectations

1. Delivery must be outstanding! The shorter the cycle or delivery time, the better we can meet our customer's needs. Suppliers' delivery performance is tracked and

based upon the want date indicated in the purchase order. We encourage suppliers to provide us copies of their own internal reports that track performance. Suppliers that have the capability to deliver directly to our in-plant end-users can significantly reduce our transaction costs. We are a dynamic company in the growth stage that challenges our suppliers with formidable delivery dates. If you can't provide us a specific part, we would expect your strong commitment in obtaining the part from another source or supplier. Lead-time reduction is essential for our continued competitive viability. As an Original Equipment Manufacturer, we have penalty clauses for late equipment delivery.

2. We want quality certified suppliers. We prefer ISO 9000 certification status or better. Inform us if you are already quality certified by other customers or industries. Give us the names and contacts of customer references that have certified you in quality. We want to know about your quality certification process. We need a thorough description of your quality program and copies of key quality documents. We are interested if you have recently received any quality-based awards. We expect that you employ a supplier-selection process that emphasizes quality. We want your quality level to be such that it eliminates the need for our internal inspection. We track a supplier's number of rejects and number of returns. We insist that suppliers correct Nonconforming Materials (NCMRs) as expeditiously as possible.

3. Back orders are an administrative nightmare for both a supplier and customer. We track the number of line items

shipped complete on the first shipment. First time "no problem" fill rates are crucial.

4. Accuracy in receiving documents is indispensable because of the accelerated pace of our growth. We track the number of packing slip errors, the number of items shipped in error, and the number of items priced incorrectly. These are administrative errors that cost us time and energy to process. Suppliers need to correct these mistakes with the minimum of disruption to us. The packing slip must have the date shipped, supplier name, invoice number, purchase-order number, shipped quantity, backorder quantity, and the part description, which includes our part number. The purchase order number must be clearly designated on the outside of the box to help us find a specific part. Other information you need to include if available is the name of the person who ordered these parts. We expect all of our suppliers to have bar-code capability. We are working with many suppliers on electronic matching strategies.

5. We expect professionalism from all our suppliers. We do a qualitative evaluation of supplier response to phone inquiries, the packing of items, ability to follow shipping instructions, and pricing competitiveness.

6. We count on "most-favored" pricing status. This means that you extend to us the lowest, best price and margins that you would grant to your very best customers. We do periodic benchmarking of pricing to verify competitive pricing. As a practice, we ask for a comprehensive, fixed price list for our parts for a period of one year. We keep a three-year history, but would expect that you work

with us to develop a history of usage and pricing. Joint updating of our contract files and computer systems is an anticipated outcome of our efforts. Written justification of any price increase is required. Price increases must be mutually agreed to by both parties. Suppliers must agree to work with us to eliminate inflationary price increases and to give us alternatives to drive down the overall supply chain costs.

7. We are interested in a turnkey approach to inventory. This would include concepts such as continuous replenishment, onsite stocking, consideration of consignment, elimination of restocking charges, recommendations around storage racks, assistance in disposing of obsolete parts, and the capability to expand the parts list that you can provide to us.

8. We need suppliers who can eliminate all transaction costs. You must have the capability to accept purchase credit cards and deal with our ERP system. EDI or electronic data exchange capability and installation expertise is a plus. We want systems-purchasing capability along with electronic mail and electronic catalogue options.

9. Our financial standard financial terms are 2-percent 15 net 60. We will not normally grant any down payments or prepayments. Our credit rating is outstanding. We require full financial disclosure of a supplier's financial status to include audited financial reports, SEC form 10K and 100, credit rating documents, and corporate financial records on file. We also insist on disclosure of any relationships with our competitors. Your price list must include each item's country of origin and reference the

original manufacturer's part number and cross-reference it to our part number. You need to make available to our assigned agent all import documentation required to facilitate a manufacturer's duty drawback. We sell internationally and expect suppliers to meet the differing language requirements of our international customers, which would include CE Mark and international-type contractual specifications.

10. We seek suppliers that can help us continuously improve. In order to encourage this behavior, we are willing to split hard improvement savings with you 50-50 for the first year of these savings. We need your help in educating end-users, designing manuals, working with cross-functional teams, and introducing new products. We want to take advantage of your technical expertise. We value suppliers with good technical services and those who can keep us informed of leading edge technologies that we can employ.

11. We are open to long-term relationships in a partnership mode. We seek long-term contracts signed with partners whenever feasible (three years or longer). Any prior track record of business and prior partner relationships is helpful. We prefer an accounting of your partnering experience along with specific contact listing of references that can verify your performance as a supplier in a partner or alliance relationship. We look forward to our suppliers educating our plant personnel on the benefits of partnering, willing to expand the bucket of goods that they can provide us, willing to engage in an onsite-supplier relationship, and agreeable to us visiting their plant and assisting us in streamlining the supply chain. The startup of a

partnership relationship is extremely resource-intensive. A supplier must dedicate resources during the startup phase.

12. We are trying to pick the "best of the best" of world-class suppliers. We want to know about any best practices that you are using. We want to know about the stability of your workforce, your commitment to progressive organizational design, and the skills of your employees. Current business capacity and future growth plans are important to help us understand your capabilities. Shutdown timing information and your status as a union or non-union manufacturer is requested.

13. We strongly urge our suppliers to conduct themselves according to the ethical standards noted by ISM Institute of Supply Management

Predictably many of them dropped out or thought that our purchasing dollars were too small to make it cost-effective for them to bother to adhere to our expectations. Then we asked those who wanted to remain to make an in-person presentation to us. A criterion was developed to help evaluate the presentations. We divided up the presentations and met and made decisions on which suppliers were we going to keep. It took much time, but the results were spectacular.

Many purchasing departments have been implementing supply-base rationalization strategies since the latter half of the 1990s in order to reduce the administrative costs associated with a large number of suppliers, to streamline purchasing processes, and to improve control over inventory. In purchasing and supply departments, supplier consolidation or supply-base rationalization continues. It is understood to mean identifying the ideal number of suppliers—a number that often turns out to be much lower than the current amount. The number often depends on industry conditions. The trend toward supplier rationalization has continued dramatically even as purchasing and supply managers have begun to contend with the possibilities and challenges presented by the rise of e-procurement, which at first glance may seem incompatible with rationalization. After all, with extensive search capabilities available through any web browser, and with the proliferation of electronic storefronts and virtual markets, e-procurement promises to open up a world of potential new suppliers that can be identified through the Internet. However, the Internet is a cold medium, and it does not necessarily improve relationships, so make sure it's used for the proper purpose.

E-procurement supports a supply-base reduction so long as the focus remains on rationalization as a strategy and on e-procurement as a tool to facilitate that strategy. The implication is that growth in the virtual marketplace could increase some organizations' supply bases. Purchasing and supply managers at several organizations currently using e-procurement systems assert that these systems will in fact support their ongoing supply-base-rationalization strategies.

Don't procrastinate. Get on with it. Slash your suppliers as soon as possible. Do not back off, or you will continue to be buried by the administration of the large number of suppliers.

Know Your Suppliers' Industry Cold

The best piece of negotiations advice I ever received was to know the capabilities of your supplier, their industry, their competitors, their cost drivers, their margins, and their capabilities better than they do! This is time consuming, but it's a powerful tool. It requires homework, digging, and flat-out work. Once a supplier realizes that you understand them, it eliminates all the negotiation game playing and posturing. You will be surprised how fast they can now focus on real issues and problem solving once they know you can't be traditionally bamboozled. You obviously can't do this with every supplier only the most important and most strategic ones. It's a powerful negotiation tactic based on knowledge not histrionics. Level the playing field with your knowledge! Roll up your sleeves, dig deep, and become an industry expert. Suppliers will be impressed with your knowledge.

Your Homework Assignment Is To Know Your Suppliers And Their Industries.

Make sure you dig up the standard industry references about industries and do your homework on which suppliers or companies are at the top in the industry. In most industries, there are three or four top companies, and although they may differ on many routine items or commodities, you can't go very wrong by picking one of the top three or four as your supplier. Don't procrastinate on these types of items.

Executive management needs to understand one important concept: Suppliers can make or break any business or business plan. According to Dr. W. Edwards Deming, defective materials or equipment—not human error or a defective process—cause over 80 percent of quality variances. Suppliers obviously play the key role in achieving high quality. Suppliers need to be treated as stakeholders, not adversaries. World-class suppliers can become a company's very best competitive weapons. They play the quintessential role in reducing time to market.

The major challenges of supply management include maximizing supplier contributions by focusing on supplier partners and on continuous improvement. The focus must be on quality, flexibility, and reducing time to market. Ultimately, company performance is judged by the paying customers or what I call the final, end-user customer. Typically, purchasing gets totally sidetracked and thinks that internal company customers are their real customers. Nothing could be further from the truth. These internal customers often whipsaw purchasing into doing stupid human tricks to satisfy their exaggerated needs.

Purchasing is not a subservient service organization at the beck and whim of internal customers. It's one of the chief revenue centers (the savings go right to the bottom line) for the corporation. It should, in conjunction with sales, find out exactly what the paying customers want—not the boisterous and misleading internal customers. Internal customers often just confuse the true end-user needs issue. Supply management professionals need to focus on what specification the ultimate paying customer wants; not the arbitrary specifications of engineering, manufacturing, shipping, or accounting. Examine if their needs actually add value. Often these internal customers are superb at defending their turf. This is one reason companies spend millions on customer research and focus groups. Many internal departments think they are the chief customers. Worse, they all think they know what the final customer wants. They are usually dead wrong, and worse yet, roadblock your discovery of the truth.

It's a good idea to administer an initial internal customers' needs-assessment checklist. It should include things like what are people's expectations from purchasing. Don't expect any major insights here. Often their expectations are mired in traditional thinking, and their self-serving, tunnel-vision requirements. Purchasing needs to understand what purchasing is evaluated on, and especially how the score is kept. Purchasing metrics are critical. Often the score is tilted to benefit internal customers. Price reductions are only 5 to 10 percent of the savings potential for a company. Hidden costs can be over 90 percent. New reporting relationships must be discussed. A new, efficient supply chain organization chart must be proposed and agreed upon in advance. Everyone needs to get more involved in the product's design—and more importantly, with sales, just in order to get to know the paying customer on a personal basis. Supply managers need to lead the charge in judiciously challenging what the customer really needs.

A customer-resource assessment is required continuously. This is not a process that can be done only sporadically. Unless the team is completely dedicated to the process, it will fail. Resistance to change will be fierce and harsh. One way to overcome the resistance is to insure that communications of changes are open and outstanding. It's important to wisely choose a very first project or supply chain task. Initial success in this project is critical for future success. Success does, in fact, snowball.

Often it's wise to pick the process that is the rift with duplicate steps and a clear, easy victory when basic streamlining is accomplished. The supply chain team must be trained in the process, and a facilitator is highly recommended. The team needs to prepare to be under attack and be aware of the rule of change.

In order to create a change in most organizations, you must adhere to what I call the seven times rule. A change must be presented seven times and explained seven different ways in order for it to start to take hold in an organization. Remember, people have distrusted purchasing or supply chain personnel for years. They will not change overnight.

Pick The Right Supplier Partners Or Else

Don't generate a boatload of partnerships or alliances with suppliers. True partnerships are deep relationships, and they must be tightly controlled and evaluated. It makes no sense to partner with hundreds of suppliers just for the sake of using the partnership term. True partnerships require major energy, relationship effort, money, and time.

One of the prime criteria for selecting a supplier as a partner is the fact that they have in fact had previous partner experience. This is a tremendous advantage and should not be discounted at all in your criteria. Think of partnering as important as a long-term marriage, and treat it as such. Divorces are very bloody, so choose your supplier-partner carefully.

Ask other companies that are partners with them how the relationship is working out, and if they are satisfied. References are critical when building relationships. In almost every consulting project that I have led, one of the key end goals was to get a strong recommendation from the client. This is especially important for future business building.

Suppliers Must Meet The Supplier Metrics

Suppliers who have had experience with non-traditional purchasing concepts, alliances, and partnerships definitely have an advantage concerning developing a deep relationship. Make sure you take the time to explain your procurement or supply chain strategy to them and to take the time to understand their strategy. They need to know what's in it for them. Make it clear and measurable. "Feeling good about each other" will not get to the bottom line. Appearances do count. You can size up a supplier's partner quotient by actual site visits and talking to their employees at all levels. Smiling faces are better than growls and disgruntled remarks. The potential future frontier with suppliers has some particular characteristics. These characteristics include most-favored customer contracts, elimination of incoming inspection, reduction of supplier base, early supplier involvement in design, value engineering, mutual cost reductions, targeting of nonproduction company costs, the complete integration of key suppliers into the business, mutual Lean and Six Sigma efforts, and extensive use of cross-functional teams. This quantum leap philosophy with suppliers requires the education of supply management personnel, rapid access to information, and supplier empowerment. Cross-functional business teams and a constant dedication to improve and to reduce time to market are key elements to look for in a potential supplier partner.

Quantum leaps are usually made by listening to the supplier and implementing their recommendations. Unfortunately, rarely do they occur from internal suggestions. Many internal employees have been beat up for years, and are risk adverse. Suppliers are the experts on their particular parts or service, not you. Heed their suggestions.

We once had a supplier recommend a simple design change on an iron casting. Not only was it cheaper, but the production line was ecstatic because it was much easier to assemble. The former appendage of the old design had often broken off during assembly.

Don't Procrastinate In The Bids Process

Always set a final deadline for returning a Request for Information (RFI) or Request for a Proposal (RFP). If a supplier does not meet the deadline, do not consider them. Don't ever compromise a bid or the bid process by favoring certain suppliers. Many folks want to procrastinate on bids. The real reason is that their stake in a relationship with their hometown supplier is threatened. They feel that they may be proven dead wrong, especially if their favorite-son supplier falters. If suppliers can't follow basic instructions on RFPs, do you really want them in a relationship? I think not. If a supplier has been the favored hometown supplier for years, do you think that they want to change? I think not.

Keep Contract Terms Simple

Why have hundreds of different and complicated terms with suppliers, contracts, and agreements? Suppliers love confusion and nonstandard approaches. Boilerplate whatever you can. Any contract that takes more than thirty days to put in place isn't worth doing. Lawyers, bureaucrats, and fools always think that somehow a contract will "protect" them or the company. Relationships are not built on the thickness of the pages of a massive contract. Trust must come first, not legal "i-dotting." He who hides behind a contract needs high life insurance. Contracts won't save you from adversarial relationships. Contracts, in fact, encourage them. *Handshakes* encourage trusting relationships.

Overthrow The Price King

Any supplier can lowball on the price of any item. I have seen it done hundreds of times. Retail stores are great at having a lead-in low-price item in one aisle with the marked up high margin items very near. Always benchmark your prices whenever possible with other companies. Keep a handle on the price pulse. When a supplier offers a lowball price on a particular part or service, see if they can extend the percent price decrease to all the other items you buy from them. Usually, dead silence results, or the quick backpedaling begins. Calling their bluff almost always works. Call it.

The Best Company Equals The Best Suppliers

The Porter model is a powerful tool that can be used in supplier selection and understanding the selection process. It's a systematic approach to market analysis that is often used by marketing. The goal here is industry analysis and to enable supply management to know as much or more about an industry as a supplier who is participating in that industry. This tool reinforces the maxim that he or she who has the most information in negotiations has the advantage. Believe it. Knowledge is power. Shoe-pounding and other adversarial tactics are okay for theater and opera, but not supply management.

Know When To Give Up On A Supplier (Fold'em)

Don't expect every market analysis or supplier selection to go smoothly. At times, market conditions are not buyer favorable, and no amount of planning, negotiations, or cooperation will yield any mutually beneficial results. Cut your losses and revisit the market at a more favorable time. Consider alternative parts or materials.

No Puffery For Savings

Leverage anything you can with a supplier. It's not just about price, but also about the services that they can provide for you. Whatever you leverage from a supplier, make sure all your folks understand what you have leveraged and consistently tell the success story across the enterprise. Keep the stories straight and consistent. Clearly differentiate tangible and non-tangible savings. Get the finance department to agree with your definitions. Don't exaggerate leverage savings. Keep them simple and understandable. Total-cost-of-ownership cost reductions can be achieved and clearly explained with diligent work.

Suppliers Can Help You Innovate, So Ask Them

Many suppliers have years of experience with many customers and have seen best practices in action. Ask them frequently for advice, and act upon it. Suppliers are one of the best sources of innovation. They do not have your corporate politics to stifle them. Many know what has worked for other companies.

CHAPTER 10:
TESTING SUPPLIERS

Always Kick Your Suppliers' Tires

Never incorporate a new supplier without a test run of buying an item from them, period. No exceptions. Have a purchasing professional pretend that he is an end-user. Have him play dumb and actually order an item from the new supplier. Review the entire transaction process to include acknowledgement and invoice payment. Carefully process-map it out, and use Lean and Six Sigma principles. Check on status often. This one road test tip will save you mountains of headaches and resistance to change. Folks do not really want new suppliers. Bad new suppliers infuriate internal customers. Remember most folks do not like change. They will latch on to any minor or frivolous mistake to justify their resistance and to castigate the new supplier.

I often required suppliers to also process map our supply chain processes so that they would gain a keen understanding of them. We did various streams to include the materials and administration. We reciprocated and visited their plants and mapped out their processes. Yes, it was time consuming, but often, it paid off. The final test of understanding was a presentation to a group. These were often mutually educational, and the details left out were corrected and, many times, creatively improved.

As a Six Sigma black belt, I was often impatient with the tedious nature of the Six Sigma process. It does work, but it requires patience and dedication. Always Lean a process first before you attempt to use Six Sigma. It's more straightforward, intuitive, visual, and the results are often very quick.

Remember many cost-saving ideas are simple "just-do-its." Don't try to label them as a Lean or Six Sigma-driven idea. Just get them done and report the savings.

Auctions Do Not Build Relationships

Suppliers view auctions as just one-time, competitive bids. To expect a strong supplier relationship out of an auction is sheer folly. Suppliers are just trying to win business at the lowest cost to them. Auctions are, at best, marginally good for keeping suppliers honest. They work best for mass commodities. Don't expect any long-term commitments from suppliers who win the auction, or any extra, added services. If you attempt to Wal-Mart your suppliers, do not expect any extra free Nordstrom-like services. You will get the Spartan treatment, which is really what you asked for by the process.

Visit Your Supplier Sites Often

You can tell much about a person by visiting their home and surroundings. This also holds true for suppliers. Check out the attitude of employees, housekeeping, professionalism, and facilities. Never ever enter a serious partnership with a supplier without visiting their main plants or facilities. Don't be afraid to go off-tour and talk to other employees. You will learn about their culture and their capabilities. Most folks are honest about whom they work for when asked in a nonthreatening manner. You will be surprised at what you learn from such conversations. Just the appearance of a factory reveals a supplier's competence. What says more is the employees' smiling!

Supplier Trial Periods Are Precarious

During supplier trial periods, new suppliers are most vulnerable to naysayers and attackers. Make sure you meet with them frequently. You need to act almost with SWAT-team efficiency when a problem occurs, and solve it immediately. Agree to problem-solving procedures and deadlines in advance. Mutually solve glitches and explain what happened openly. This is not the time for shoving things under the rug or stonewalling problems. Fix them on the spot whenever possible. When you are at fault for the misunderstanding, admit it openly.

Supplier D-I-V-O-R-C-E Is Tough For Many

Many end-users have personal stakeholder relationships in certain suppliers and the relationships developed over the years with these suppliers. A transformation plan must be established to deal with the adjustment to new relationships with new suppliers. Use a change-management model to address these issues and guarantee the acceptance of any e-procurement initiative. Breaking up is hard to do, as the song says, but it must be done and done quickly. Many buyers cannot stay objective when dealing with a long-term supplier. Give them a chance but stay objective and open to new suppliers.

If You Select the Wrong Supplier, Fess Up Quickly

It's painful and expensive, but you must shoot that bad supplier racehorse immediately if the fit is not there. Usually when the strategic selection process is short-circuited or not fully employed, a supplier mistake is made. Many people on collaborative supplier-selection teams get impatient and push for a quick decision. Supplier-selection mistakes are more the fault of not doing the homework or following the process. Other failure causes include the inability to establish a true relationship. Again, this is a hard process to predict or quantify. Admit the mistake, finalize the divorce, and then reexamine the process of selection. Deselect, then reselect. Get over it.

CHAPTER 11:
SOURCING SUPPLIERS

Retraining Supply Management Professionals, And Why Bids Are Way Overrated

Unfortunately, many supply chain professionals do not want to learn new approaches or non-traditional purchasing or supply management techniques. The key is to train them to relate to suppliers and customers. No matter what you try, if they do not believe in the process in their heart, they will not change.

It's hard to teach trust, integrity, or character. These above all else are necessary for supply chain professionals. Traditional purchasing rewards the exact wrong skills and behaviors. It rewards pencil pushers and mindless bureaucrats. Requirements are basically dictated or thrown over the wall to purchasing, who often select a supplier by a rigid, low-cost bid process. Ironically, most non-purchasing employees think the bid process somehow protects a company and is honest. Purchasing professionals soon realize the exact opposite is true. It is a process swimming with danger and dishonesty. Price is often the mindless king. *Cheap* is regarded as *better*.

The purchasing or supply management department is often heavily transaction focused, with multiple and complicated steps just to purchase an item, no matter how small or cheap. Redundancy is rampant. Requisitions drive the workload, and pedantic rules inhibit any real relationships with suppliers. Customer needs go right out the window, and procedures, bids, and contracts rule.

Progressive supply management is highly team-oriented—especially cross-functional teams. The examination of the supply chain and total cost of ownership drives the decision-making process. There is a systematic process for supplier selection. Relationship building and management is the key skill for the purchasing professional. When senior management not only supports but also understands the process, purchasing becomes a true business partner and leader.

Total cost of ownership is a tough concept to teach. Do *not* give up...teach it! I often gave seminars on it. People often laser in on price simply because it's an easy concept to compare. I used an example of personal computers. Hardware costs are interesting and often close, but they should not drive the decisions. By far, the critical costs are system and software maintenance. They can bog down and destroy an IT department forever. Automobiles can also have high maintenance and repair costs over their lifespan. Although the user should have a key say in many decisions, the people who have to maintain the part or product are critical to understanding the total cost of ownership. Never leave the maintainers out of your decision team. They are refreshingly honest in their evaluations—especially when they realize that they will have to maintain the product or service.

Be Methodical In Sourcing

There are many comprehensive-sourcing or supplier-selection models available. Most require careful research and a team approach. Remember these are meant for important suppliers, materials or services—those that have a big impact on the bottom line. Don't waste time on such a thorough process for routine purchases. Strategic sourcing is a disciplined process that organizations implement in order to more efficiently purchase goods and services from suppliers. The goal is to reduce total-acquisition cost while improving value. Forrester research has reported that 40 percent of the total reductions in costs are associated with technology, while the other 60 percent are associated with strategic-sourcing techniques. Here are my five key points to jumpstart strategic sourcing:

- Understand the state of your current spending (not always easy).

- Prepare a sourcing strategy for particular commodities, and tie the strategy into your business strategy, mission, or vision.

- Evaluate the current competencies of your suppliers and how to extract value from these sources.

- Decide what's important for you in your sourcing strategy and how it relates to selecting your possible technology solution.

- Always do a risk assessment.

Limit Strategic Suppliers And The Sourcing-Process Timeline

Strategic sourcing is a disciplined process organizations implement in order to purchase goods and services from suppliers more efficiently. The goal is to reduce total-acquisition cost while improving value. A strategic sourcing strategy should be initiated immediately—especially for key cost items. A comprehensive sourcing methodology should be followed religiously to include strategic alliance and strategic relationship building with key suppliers. Key supplier alliances must be established. Supplier rationalization (reduction) must be accomplished first, however, and dramatically. Many consulting firms offer a strategic-sourcing management solution that walks online users through each step of a consulting-type procurement methodology, including gathering data, analyzing requirements, and setting strategy, as well as executing e-procurement through shopping e-marketplaces, conducting reverse auctions, and using other methods built into the application. Don't reinvent it; use their template.

Here is a basic strategic-sourcing six-step process:

- Assess Opportunity.

- Assess Internal Supply Chain.

- Assess Supply Markets.

- Develop Sourcing Strategy.

- Implement Strategy.

- Institutionalize Strategy.

The activities within each step may appear to be performed in sequence, but in fact, *they are not*. This is not a linear process, but rather, a complicated and simultaneous one. Over the course of the process, the sourcing teams may often revisit the steps and revise their approaches.

Here are just some of the noted key benefits to addressing strategic sourcing and procurement:

- Reduction of overall costs equals centralized, negotiated contracts and a streamlined procurement process that takes advantage of all available discounts.

- Increased communications about products equals improved use of technology.

- A reduced number of suppliers equals stronger relationships/partnerships with suppliers, resulting in a more-flexible and responsive supply pipeline that is managed proactively instead of reactively.

- Increased purchasing efficiency equals use of e-commerce applications and procurement cards.

- Reduced purchased-unit costs.

- Reduced acquisition costs.

- Increased inventory turnover.

- Improved downstream operations equal higher quality shipments, on time—the right components in the right quantities.

Supplier alliances or partnerships remain critical for any supply chain success. In addition the e-procurement readiness for these suppliers must be assessed rigorously and tested. All too often suppliers exaggerate their e-procurement or digital capabilities. You must insist on the actual testing of supplier e-procurement and electronic catalogue capabilities. Suppliers must be assessed to see if they are ready for e-procurement. Capabilities must be measured and actual references from other companies sought out to insure that the chosen suppliers could deal with e-procurement. Strong consideration should be given to dividing or segmenting suppliers into tiers of capability such as Tiers 1-2-3. Supplier integration with back office systems is also a strong criterion. Alliances should only be formed with suppliers who can offer some sort of a significant competitive edge or who cover and reduce major purchasing dollars.

The supplier relationship is where the traditional and the progressive purchasing differ the most. The traditional is a short term approach, adversary-based and mostly hands off commercial. Serious cost cutting is rare. Communication is usually at arm's length. Shopping is a continuous charade and purchasing is perpetually hunting for a better ""deal." The world is one big strip mall of suppliers. The low bidder often wins the bid. The norm is three quotes and the required blizzard of paperwork for a cheap supplier. The atmosphere is one of low trust, weak commitment, and supplier long-term performance is often not monitored well. Expediting of parts is a continuous three-ring circus.

More modern supplier relationships are geared toward the long term—at least three to five years. Close collaboration is open, with the mutual sharing of plans, design, goals, and rewards. The lowest total cost of ownership is valued, and value-adding services are the norm. Suppliers are empowered to just *get it done*.

Ramming The Iceberg

The Iceberg of Supplier Opportunity theory holds that only five to ten percent of efficiency is gained via price, and it's the area of least resistance and work. The ninety to ninety-five percent (hidden costs) of the so-called new frontier of supplier exploration is bottom-line, total-cost-of-ownership savings of using a preferred supplier. This is the one area of the greatest resistance and opportunity. This is the realm of relationship building that requires increasing communication and the building of trust. Flexibility in supplier relationship building is a must. Use the 80-20 rule. Concentrate on building relationships with the suppliers with whom you spend the most dollars. Only develop relationships with suppliers who will give you a distinct competitive advantage that directly impacts your paying or end-user customers. Most corporations can only manage a few of these critical relationships. They must be at the highest level, with executive and other personnel exchanges. Thus many low-value or miscellaneous materials do not really need strong relationship efforts. These relationships can remain strictly commercial. There is no need to waste precious resources on developing relationships with these suppliers. Beware of hot issue materials. Steer clear of the emotional materials at first. Many people in companies develop personal relationships with suppliers. Note that people love trinkets, dinners, golf, and personal attention from suppliers. Unfortunately, this doesn't drive money to the company's bottom line. Don't underestimate this personal factor.

More Thoughts On Transformation

Identify your key suppliers early. If anyone in your organization has had prior transformation experience, use him or her as much as possible especially in supplier selection. Transformation is often an endurance contest where the last man or woman (gladiator) left standing wins. The problem is that many individuals dig in and hope to wear the strategic-sourcing team out. Sourcing is a marathon, not a sprint. Don't be afraid to lose some minor battles initially in order to win the war. The long haul is a long haul. Remember the needs of paying customers must drive the process. Note or list internal customer needs only. Concentrate on what counts to the ultimate paying customers. How do we find this out? Ask them! Supplier receptiveness to the relationships and the change process needs to be carefully and slowly thought out. Top management needs to understand that resistance will be fierce and some individuals will not change and must be dealt with appropriately.

Keep Score Creatively

Accounting needs to rethink the way it keeps score. Standard cost-based systems are too antiquated to adequately report on progress for this process. Activity-based accounting is much more suited to the process, and the correct assessment of progress. Always strive for the highest performance with clear vision and clear objectives. Internal customers or end-users that previously were not permitted to perform transactions or even dialogue with suppliers now must be seamlessly connected. Supply management must get out of the worthless middle-person role syndrome that they have historically played. Supply management needs to bury its role as a rule-throwing, contract rule imbedding, and innovation obstructionists. The organization must constantly be flexible and look forward to upgrades. Markets change; so must supply management. Get on your track shoes and keep ahead of the market.

Standardize Whatever You Can

Engineers always have their own pets and biases. We all do. It's critical to get them on cross-functional teams to standardize parts and equipment. A goal of 80-percent standardized parts is realistic in many industries. Differences in brands (suppliers), Original Equipment Manufacturers (OEMs), and parts must have significant added value to be justified.

Why is standardization important? Try to measure quality with an obscure balkanization of OEMs and different parts. Good luck. The same holds for services: standardize them. One of the guiding principles of industrialization is standardization. Don't lose sight of it! Pursue it. Standardize whenever possible.

Total-Cost-Of-Ownership Education Takes Effort

Most folks do not understand total cost of ownership or concepts like activity-based costing. They are still mired in the "price-is-king" world. They can't get past price. Always visually process map the total cost of a supply chain—especially if resistance to change is strong. Try to calculate the costs of various steps, transformations, and non-value-added stuff. Do your research. Explain total costs.

CHAPTER 12:
SUPPLY MANAGEMENT METRICS

The Right Metrics Produce the Right Results

Success in reducing cycle time can be readily measured both quantifiably and qualitatively. However, obviously, baselines should be established before any measurements of success or outcomes can be performed. Here are some of my suggestions for effective cycle-time measurements:

- **On-Time Delivery**
  Enhanced methods to measure on-time delivery include separating components into "A," "B," and "C," categories ("A" being the top priority). Strategic materials must arrive on time. The non-strategic material deliveries should be tracked differently. Their purpose is an ancillary support- ing role with more delivery leeway being tolerated. To distinguish these categories of delivery, many companies break delivery performance down into these "A," "B," and "C" categories with different percentage goals in each category. One non-traditional measurement is the number of "no-hitch" or perfect deliveries. This means a smooth delivery with zero redundancies and no extra non-value-adding work.

- **Inventory Reduction Measurements**
  Measure improved inventory accuracy, labor hours saved taking inventory, elimination of racks, shelves, and

materials handling equipment, and reduced maintenance costs. Don't stop here. Many suppliers readily agree to hold materials on a consignment basis. This is a valuable cost-avoidance and cash-flow improvement. Whenever possible, drive to get agreement to pay on consumption. Track reductions in supplier inventory. This will help them reduce or hold down their costs to you. Measure inventory committed to by suppliers and the value of materials now on consignment or on pay-on-consumption systems. Make note of the various functions or departments that are outsourced. Obtain realistic estimates of the amount of inventory and overhead that would have been required to support these activities if they were not outsourced.

- **Increase-in-Inventory Turnover**
  Focus your efforts on the "one-touch theory" and the "speed to point of use" for materials or services. Track the number of materials or services touched by only one person in the process right at the point of use or where they are directly needed. Count the total number of transactions processed directly by the end-user without any purchasing or middleman interface. A bonus would be that they arrive directly to the end-user precisely at the point of use in the manufacturing process. Measure the time it takes for all materials or services to hit your property and get to the point of use.

- **Decrease in Total Cost of Ownership**
  Identify your cost drivers first. These are your significant cost factors that drive the cost of a material or service. Then concentrate on the costs usually reduced or eliminated by faster cycle time but often forgotten in the rush.

Measure areas in which processes got simpler and training costs were decreased.

- **Visibility and Appreciation**

  Measure the number of cross-functional teams that purchasing participates in and leads. These can be broken down into three general arenas: design, process, and administrative. Keep records of the number of times other departments come to your department to seek input, advice, and basic participation on strategic planning. Track the number of suppliers that add value to your products at the design stage and the results of their efforts.

- **Increased Integration of Purchasing Strategy into Corporate Strategy**

  Create a five-year strategic plan for purchasing and integrate it into the company's overall strategic plan. Get out into the field with sales and marketing to find out what the final customer really wants in your product, and get the materials and services to meet these needs. Keep track of the number of final customer contacts and the number of changes made because of their input.

- **Increased Cooperation from Suppliers**

  Document all supplier-driven innovations and improvements. Increase and document the number and type of direct links with suppliers, especially direct electronic ties to your production schedule and EDI. Develop in-depth alliance relationships with a few key suppliers at a strategic level to make your quantum leaps in cycle-time reduction. Then measure the success of the alliance by measuring the reduced cycle time. Survey your key suppliers and ask them what they think of the progress of the alliances.

- **Decrease in Manufacturing-Cycle Time**
  Keep the tracking of this key parameter simple, to the point, and at a macro level. Show the number of widgets made compared to the cost of goods sold. Thus, if you cut cycle time by 50 percent, you should make approximately twice as many widgets with about the same cost of goods sold. Realistically, the cost of goods sold will have to increase, but cycle-time reduction can radically hold down the rate of increase.

- **Purchasing's Internal Customer-Client Satisfaction**
  Start an ongoing internal customer focus team to evaluate the performance and service of purchasing. Periodically use surveys of internal customers, final customers, and suppliers to obtain valuable feedback and direction on how to reduce cycle time. Always include in customer-satisfaction surveys the question, "Has the response time to your request increased, decreased, or stayed the same?" Don't forget face-to-face feedback meetings.

- **Manufacturing Flexibility**
  When measuring flexibility in the manufacturing process, focus on reducing the total number of parts. Purchasers can track increases in the number of easily obtainable standardized parts and services with zero lead-time. Suppliers can preassemble and assist in these types of efforts.

Don't neglect the administrative-cycle time in a purchasing department—whether you work for a manufacturing company or a service organization. Purchasers can set cycle-time standards in their departments and streamline all procedures to speed things up. For example, procurement cards and system-purchasing can help reduce cycle time. With these ten measurements, your efforts to reduce cycle time will become focused and can be easily understood by your customers and suppliers. Use them as much as is feasible. Lean and Six Sigma are also great tools.

If you can't measure it, why in the heck are you doing it?

Some Of My Additional Possible Nontraditional Measures For Procurement To Be Noted:

- The number of preferred suppliers under long-term contract.

- The number of supplier-alliance relationships.

- The number of single-source parts, commodities, services.

- The number of suppliers providing onsite service.

- The number of new products or design reviews that suppliers participated in on a team.

- The number of transactions processed directly by the end-user.

- The number and dollar-value of mutual cost reductions with suppliers.

- The number and dollar-volume of purchase-card purchases or electronic purchases.

- The number of cross-functional teams on which purchasing professionals are contributing members.

- The dollar value on continuous-replenishment stocking plans.

- The percentage of supply chain personnel pursuing an advanced degree.

- The number of continuing-education hours or seminar hours taken supply chain personnel.

- The percentage of supply chain professionals certified.

- The number of suppliers registered to ISO-9000.

- The number of suppliers with direct links to you.

- The number of active suppliers.

- The average lead-time of purchased components and parts.

- The cycle time or velocity of delivery of our equipment to the customer. Process speed or efficiency.

- Cycle time from sales-order placement to purchased-part acquisition.

- Creation and updating of a five-year strategic purchasing plan.

- Effective use of social networks in relationship building.

There are more than enough significant metrics and justification available for non-traditional procurement. The challenge is selling the concept to top management. Usually and unfortunately, they are much more interested in bottom line impacts for the next quarterly report.

Keep It Visible, Clear, And Simple.

Show folks how you are doing versus your metrics. Use pictures and graphics. People can relate to them much better. Spreadsheets are not very publicity friendly. Don't be shy with graphs, and always display them professionally. Keep the radar gun on the process and suppliers. Let other folks see the results, good and bad.

One of the fundamental tenets of Lean is visibility. Use it in supply management.

Aim High With People's Standards

Set the standards of performance for yourself and your people high. Expectation-setting is critical to success. Reward outstanding performance, not average performance. Encourage purchasing professionals to become experts in a market, industry, or supplier group. Most of all, encourage them to know your business, the cost drivers, and the end-customer's needs, and strive to exceed them.

CHAPTER 13:
DISCIPLINE AND RULES

Provide Consequences For Bad Crows And Enforce The Rules

Governance, rules, and discipline in buying are essential. Folks that violate the rules must be dealt with quickly, and the workforce needs to realize the consequences. Again, the first crows that jump off the fence need to be taken care of quickly. Put the weapon on auto-fire. *Kapow!* Maverick buying will soon dry up.

Discipline Without Enforcement Isn't

Purchasing, supply management, and transaction discipline are critical. Most folks do not like it, but most of the routine purchases and process must be disciplined. Discipline—especially around using preferred suppliers—must be strictly enforced. Make folks e-savvy and adept at using catalogues. Teach them how to search catalogues, or they will soon quit searching.

Pay Supply Management Folks For Performance

Pay supply management folks on how well they do with their commodities, materials, or services. They must beat the market they are dealing with. If the market prices went down 5-percent during the year, they need to do better than a 5-percent price reduction. Make them market-focused first. Don't make them focus on bureaucratic stuff.

Firefighters Don't Model The Desired Behavior

Crisis victims love good firefighters. If supply management folks are involved in too many tactical firefights, they aren't doing their jobs—especially strategically—or they have chosen the wrong suppliers. Don't reward good firefighters; it just encourages short-term, firefighting behavior. Prevention of fires must be valued. Ask Smokey the Bear. He will concur.

CHAPTER 14:
BUREAUCRACY

Eliminate Or Simplify Transactions

Face it, internal folks view doing their procurement transactions as an outright pain in the neck. Every effort must be made to make them simple, intuitive, and painless. Catalogues must be super-simple. Catalogue content is a key. Time is of the essence to anyone buying. One of the reasons the Russian empire fell was not Star Wars, but because so many people had to wait so long in so many lines in order to buy so few basically worthless goods. Waiting really riles people up. Target a transaction completion for thirty seconds or less. If you can archive previous requisitions that folks can copy, cut, and paste quickly into new ones, by all means, employ this tactic. Don't waste their time on busywork. Their time is valuable.

Do Not Bake A Bureaucratic Layer Cake

Don't add layers of audits, logs, paperwork, and other drivel to simple routine buys, for Pete's sake. Most of this stuff is not necessary for folks to do their jobs. Don't add layers of bureaucracy to "protect" the company. Small purchase orders are small, chump-change stuff. Concentrate on the strategic items. This is where the folding money is. Many companies have many restrictions on small-dollar-value transactions that do not make sense. They bend over to pick up the pennies while the paper bills or folding money flies right away. Let it go. Trust your employees to do small purchase orders.

Bureaucracy's Vampire Heart Needs A Stake In It

Bureaucracy can never be successfully downsized or reduced—it must be obliterated with a passion, or it will come back with a vengeance and re-entrench itself. Take no prisoners. Salt the bureaucracy earth. Don't modify or adjust it…*destroy it.*

Tantrums Require Strong Rebukes From Grownups

As with kids, use timeouts for the screamers. Make sure you explain that you will not tolerate such tactics. Don't be afraid to walk out of a meeting when they are used. Confront the behavior first, and do not tolerate it. If it persists, pull the trigger.

Bean Counters Need Corrective Medicine

Many accountants can't get beyond price. Their accounting systems can't measure soft or activity-based costs. They always want to see so-called hard results. They like to audit incessantly. Don't let them rule. Keep pushing back on their logic and justification. No one ever brought a share of stock because of so-called world-class accounting systems—at least I haven't.

Audits Need Cost-Benefit Analysis

Do not agree to any additional audits or audit tactics. Make auditors justify their additional audit requirements by proving how much money it will save or value it will add. No justification, no audit. *Does it save anything? Prove it.*

The Supply Managers' Fifth-Column Saboteur Effect

By far, the biggest barrier to transforming purchasing into supply management is the enormous and overwhelming fear of change. Dr. Demming was right when he cited the need to drive out fear. A severe job-security issue among purchasing professionals often helps create an atmosphere of fear that is nearly impossible to overcome. Before the undertaking of the journey of transformation of purchasing, an assessment of where purchasing professionals are on their career path and in their approach is essential. The four milestones along the path are beginners or start-up, adapters or maintenance, risk-takers or innovators, and visionary or leading edge. Purchasing or supply management professionals can be classified as reactive, mechanical, proactive, and American *Keirestsu*. The reactive state is the typical firefighting, jumping-to-operating, crisis mode of many departments. The mechanical mode is the super bureaucrat who has mastered the inefficient system. The proactive state shows spurts of planning and some significant progress. Often, it's haphazard. The American *Keirestu* is the end state of supply management prowess. The key here is to re-skill people and provide the training to lead the transformation process.

End-users (internal buyers) demand ease of use, and they want to quickly find the items that they need. Companies need to realize that e-procurement is competing with the easiest method to buy in the minds of their end-users. Many end-users would rather pick up a phone, tell their supplier what items they want, charge it to a corporate purchase card, and hang up. They would also rather buy it online quickly. Unfortunately, in many companies, this method is still faster than using some of the current software. Any impediments to the fast purchase of materials will quickly turn off end-users and kill transaction volumes. Speed is king in the world of supply management. End-users also want powerful search engines to quickly find their items. If the content-supplier catalogue is poorly organized, and the quality is poor, end-users will quickly be frustrated by unfruitful searches and become non-users of the supply management system. In addition, special instructions that need to be given to suppliers about delivery or other issues can't easily be given with some e-procurement tools, or require additional end-user training, which raises the frustration levels.

Finally, there is the relationship factor with new suppliers. Often new suppliers are installed for indirect materials solely because they seem to have more e-procurement capabilities. End-users value relationships with suppliers that they have trusted over the years. Electronic supply management is highly impersonal and web-based. Resistance to change for a software system is fierce, but it can be readily overcome with strong commitment to change management. This change-management process must be an integral part of any electronic supply management installation. Never underestimate the role resistance to change plays in this transformation. There are three sayings to be aware of when electronic supply management is implemented:

Shift Happens.

Change is Constant.

Emotion Rules Logic.

Lawyers Need Limits

Lawyers are good delayers of contracts. They love to play tit for tat with suppliers. Get them involved in boiler-plating contracts for various goods and services. Hold them to page and word limits for contracts. Make sure common sense language prevails—not legalese.

CHAPTER 15:
E-STUFF

I have provided some advice and checklists for selecting the right e-tools in this chapter. These are meant as general roadmaps and guidelines for the supply management professional.

Select The Right E-Tools

Here are some pertinent tips on selecting e-tools:

- Research all the alternatives. Potential solutions include a variety of alternatives: Internet, Intranet, extranet, application service provider (ASP), server-based, ERP, stand-alone, exchanges, and B2B hubs. Find an industry source that is not vested in the ultimate decision choice, and use its knowledge to develop the list of viable alternatives.

- Define points of integration. Working with IT and relevant support units defines those potential points of integration necessary to capitalize on information and systems investments already made. Some examples include human resources, general ledger, accounts payable, fixed assets, inventory, asset management, and help-desk applications.

- Document business needs. The ideal solution for each organization may differ, based upon the activities planned to flow through the system, commodities and services to be acquired, business practices, industry and legacy system requirements, and department or initiative budgets.

- Issue a request for information (RFI). Use the submissions to gain a much greater understanding of the offerings available in the marketplace, and to refine the system requirements.

- Eliminate unacceptable options. Drop from consideration any option that does not fall within acceptable IT parameters. If the proposed solution is incompatible with the organization infrastructure or business objectives, eliminate it. Focus on solutions that require minimal effort to integrate effectively within the planned environment.

Why Try E-Supply Management Or E-Procurement?

A company must focus on its current business or procurement practices first, before trying e-procurement. For many companies, these remain very archaic and transaction-intensive. The process of the transformation of purchasing into supply management is an excellent first step in achieving the full benefits of e-procurement. This is where a comprehensive supply management assessment is mandatory (the "as-is" state). Companies can do a gap analysis and offer a spend assessment to help in this area. Standardized purchasing processes and rules are essential preceding steps. Procurement procedures should be clearly defined, along with current supplier-relationship depth. E-procurement is a powerful tool, but a disciplined procurement approach should be in place before e-procurement solutions are implemented. The procurement must come before the e. Unfortunately, many companies do not have good information on procurement spend, transactions, commodities, and suppliers, which makes an assessment extremely difficult.

Before establishing metrics and justification for e-procurement, a familiarity with supply chain best practices must be established. Some supply chain best practices include the measurements from the following bullets:

- Form strategic alliances with suppliers, service vendors, and shippers.

- Facilitate information sharing by giving them input in strategies, plans, and product development.

- Facilitate greater information sharing of demand, product design, and development data at multiple levels of the organization.

- Reduce the number of regular suppliers by shifting to single sourcing to shorten cycle times for development and to cut costs.

- Review suppliers' performance on multiple criteria, such as ISO9000 and Malcolm Baldrige, as well as process criteria.

- Implement VMI (Vendor Managed Inventory)—the automatic or continuous replenishment of a customer's inventory by the supplier, based on product-stocking model parameters and POS data.

- Change working attitude from an adversarial relationship to a partnership relationship.

- Process is completely electronic—many companies have links with customers and suppliers and within company between systems.

- Tools to allow understanding of tradeoffs for investment buying (carrying costs, algorithms, etc.).

- Provide demand information to suppliers (i.e., consumer demand as well as customer demand).

- Strong relationship with few suppliers.

- Consolidation.

- Leveraged buying.

- Intranet-based catalogs.

- Internet-based purchasing.

- Procurement cards.

Specific E-Procurement Justification Metrics

Consider these metrics:

- *Reducing* the time employees spend purchasing, whether they're leafing through catalogues or surfing the web.

- *Leveraging* their volume with preferred suppliers in order to get better pricing, service, and access to new technology.

- *Limiting* choices to only those suppliers, materials, and services that they are confident can meet pre-approved levels of price and quality.

- An additional benefit of these approaches is reducing cycle times for responding to ongoing or unanticipated business needs. In many companies, the total elapsed time required to requisition even standard items is often weeks—resulting in manufacturing downtime or inefficiency while waiting for materials, or carrying higher buffer stocks of "just in case" inventories. Using e-procurement tools to streamline and speed up the process, these cycle times can typically be reduced to a matter of days or even hours. For efficiency-related changes, the direct impact on the bottom line is often hard to measure. For example, purchasing and administrative overhead costs really only decrease if total staff levels are reduced. If all you do is cut the number of purchase orders in half and leave your staffing at the same level, then the cost to process each simply goes up from $200 to $400. More frequently, staffs are reassigned to projects and activities that have higher potential value to the company but were previously not addressed.

Determining the real business value of these efficiency-related e-procurement solutions requires asking the question, "What new things are we doing now that we are freed from this administrative burden, and what is the measurable value to the organization?" Frankly, the answer is often not well- known or not really planned out.

Additional Benefits Checklist For E-Procurement

Examine these additional possible benefits:

- Improve productivity organization-wide through stream-lining the purchasing process and reducing cycle times. Reported results include 50-to-70-percent improvement in cycle times from an average of 7.3 days for fulfillment to two days.

- Faster cycle times eliminate the need for inventory of nearly all maintenance, repair, and operating items, reducing storage costs.

- Increases accountability of operating departments for purchasing decisions by transferring the purchasing power from the supply management department to the employee ordering the product.

- Reduces maverick buying. Many organizations have "preferred" contracts in place through which significant savings are negotiated relative to "list" pricing. Industry averages suggest 20-to-25-percent premiums are paid for "off-contract" purchasing. Implementation of a comprehensive e-procurement solution empowers an organization to manage the leakage off the contracts far more easily. If just 10 percent of the buy is moved on-contract as a result of the control and reporting available within these solutions, an organization could reduce expenses off the top by 2 to 2.5 percent.

- Creates closer collaboration between the organization and preferred providers. With automated links directing the buy, and detailed data available regarding products purchased, received, and invoiced, organizations are better prepared to manage supplier relationships effectively.

- Increases corporate leverage. With the reporting available within the systems, organizations can determine exactly how much they are spending with various suppliers for similar commodities. This knowledge can be tremendously powerful when contracts are up for renegotiation. Organizations can prove how much was spent and can guarantee that the spend will go to the selected supplier.

Content Counts The Most

Rich content drives supply management decisions, giving buyers the ability to search for products across multiple vendors and to apply complex filters to find items that meet the buyers' exact needs, enabling them to make better and faster purchasing decisions. Moreover, catalogues allow sellers to differentiate their products through rich-commerce-ready product content and participate in multiple e-marketplaces without losing control of their pricing, inventory, or discounting models. To be successful, today's net market makers must deliver rich content to attract and satisfy their diverse buyer and supplier communities.

What is rich content?

Rich content is e-commerce-ready product information (part number, description, supplier ratings, pricing, warranty, service info, etc.) that enables buyers to make better and faster purchasing decisions. Some product information, such as descriptions, may be static, while other information, such as price and availability, may change constantly.

What Are The Content Challenges?

Several challenges associated with content management limit the scalability of B2B e-commerce and e-marketplaces:

- Heterogeneous data sources such as ERP systems, relational databases, flat files, and web stores.

- Diverse supplier terminology.

- Incomplete product information.

- Dynamic information such as pricing and availability.

- Limited automation tools.

- Poor content quality.

- Lack of standards.

Rich content impacts e-procurement as follows:

Buyer or End-User Impact

- Better and faster purchasing decision.

- Improved sourcing capabilities.

- Comparison shopping.

- Ease of use ("ease of finding").

- Reduced costs.

- Single content source.

Supplier Impact

- Improved content presentation ("differentiation").

- Ability to offer enhanced information about products.

- Dramatically expand sales channel.

Selecting An E-Procurement Provider

Here is a general guide to select an e-procurement provider:

Develop a Request for Proposal: Once a short list has been developed identifying a select group of suppliers who appear to be able to meet the organizational objectives, develop a detailed request for proposal (RFP). This allows an organization to drill down and obtain specific information regarding each offering. This should include information regarding not only what they offer, but also how they offer it.

- Premise: Focus on each bidder's ability to provide a solution that achieves the desired objectives. Avoid the trap of specifying how to reach them.

- Requirements: Mandate that bidders define how the current version will meet the objectives. Be wary of optional features, future-release promises, and customization offers. There is a big difference between "We can do that," "We do that," and "We do that now."

- Infrastructure: Obtain architecture and database diagrams, system requirements for servers and desktops, network capacity implications, remote-access solutions and methods, and the number of firewall penetrations.

- Integration: Require full definition of not only what systems they will integrate, but also how they will do so, and if they have done so before.

- Suppliers: Without suppliers, an organization's e-procurement solution will be a failure. Although it may not be the most significant concern, it's a critical one. Evaluate the solution from the supplier's viewpoint. Focus on issues of cost, difficulty of integration, resource requirements to support the implementation in an ongoing fashion, and how large the supplier base is that has already been enabled for other organizations.

- Future direction: In an environment changing as quickly as this one, it's important to acknowledge that supply managers are buying the organization and its continued commitment to develop and enhance the solution as much as the technology. Understand the organization's source of funding, how much is invested in research and development in this particular application, future plans for enhancements of the system already on the drawing board, and whether and how clients influence future enhancements.

- *Assess the Products:* Assess the offering in total, including detail on the organization that is bidding. Although the size and strength of the players in the market differ greatly, the driving factor in the final analysis is capability and functionality of the systems.

- Scalability and flexibility: Assess the system's ability to scale beyond the organization of today to the organization of tomorrow. Ensure that it's flexible and scalable enough to accommodate significant growth through mergers or internal development and that it's not limited by global boundaries in its ability to support the future environment.

- Back-end functionality: Process savings generated by automation of back-end connections to financial systems will account for much of the hard-dollar savings. It's critical to assess how smooth the integration will be for the financial and reporting systems of buyers and, where relevant, suppliers.

- Ease of use: Without question, if the system is difficult to use, the bulk of the population will gravitate toward a method that is easier. Success is dependent upon implementation of a user-friendly interface that encourages desired behaviors and has rapid response times. Additionally, if significant training is required, it adds time and expense to any implementation and diminishes the likelihood of success.

- Customization: This is a double-edged sword. A system that can meet operational needs with minimal customization is likely to be a much better choice than one that requires a tremendous amount of changes. The more sophisticated the organization, the less likely it will be that a vanilla implementation of any solution will address every need. Strive to find a system that can resolve critical issues through configuration during implementation, not customization of code.

- Performance: Bypass the marketing hype. Determine how many systems are operating and processing transaction activity to multiple suppliers from multiple business units. How are they working? Were the implementations relatively straightforward, or extremely difficult? How similar are those implementations to what the organization's specific objectives are? Does it really do what it was promised to do by the sales team?

How To Analyze The Cost Of E-Procurement

Here are some ways to analyze the cost: Despite the level of investment that may be required to implement any one of the alternatives under consideration, the cost of the actual software license is often a fraction of the total cost of the decision. In developing the pricing matrix and analysis, it's imperative to assess the total cost of the decision.

- License fee: Although not always the largest percentage of the cost, the license fee can be a significant investment.

Have the bidders clearly define list price, discount off list price, how long the price is valid, and what is included within the base licensing fee.

- Subscription fee: In the event one chooses to outsource the acquisition of the product to an outside provider and pay for the rights to use the system on a subscription basis, there may be no upfront license fee charged, but there will be ongoing subscription fees. Be certain to obtain fixed quotes for a reasonable period, with caps on the providers' ability to increase those rates once the fixed quote has expired.

- Fee composition: Understand how the fee is computed. Run sensitivity analysis to determine under what scenarios, and at what points, additional charges will be incurred. Pricing methods vary widely from price per user, to number or value of transactions processed, to site licenses, and many combinations thereof. As a result, it's often difficult to complete a fair comparison of solutions using different pricing mechanisms.

- Authorized users: Be careful to clearly define what parts of the organization are covered under the agreement. Does it include subsidiaries, parent affiliates, and even subcontractors or other partner organizations? What happens if the organization buys another organization? What happens if it sells part of the existing organization?

- Annual support and maintenance fees: Typically, maintenance is priced on a percentage of prices paid for the license or service. Clearly define the percentage, under what circumstances that percentage may rise (and by how much), and on what basis the percentage is calculated for current and future acquisitions.

- Costs of upgrades: An organization's best leverage is during the initial procurement decision. Now is the time to negotiate specific pricing for future upgrades. If a fixed quote is unobtainable, at minimum, negotiate a committed discount off of the list price.

- Consulting costs for implementation: Clearly scope out the expected deliverable for a comprehensive installation and implementation of the solution into the environment. Be wary of vague estimates based on general project plans. Provide the bidders sufficient information regarding the current and future proposed environment so that they will be able to develop organization-specific estimates. Negotiate the hourly rates as well as incentive arrangements and expenses.

- Internal costs: Include all relevant costs, such as time for internal resources to implement and integrate the system initially, and manage and administer the system going forward. Calculate the hard-dollar costs to upgrade the internal network, desktop, and server hardware as necessary to support the new system.

- Other third-party costs: Don't forget to compute the costs that will be incurred if the system needs to integrate to other third-party systems, and what fees are incurred by those third-party providers to support the development of system-specific feeds or bridges.

Conducting An E-Procurement Reality Test

All too often, the differences between what suppliers can demonstrate and what the system is capable of doing are significant. At times, it's as simple as a misunderstanding relative to the intent of the question asked in the RFP. Nearly every system can do things with sufficient customization. Whether it does it as a matter of course or as part of the base package, is of concern to the evaluators.

- Hold a scripted demonstration: Require each bidder to demonstrate specific functionality that meets the business requirements defined early in the process. Have them demonstrate the steps that it takes to make certain processes happen. Focus on functions and activities that will be performed by end-users, power users, and system-administration staff to get a comprehensive picture of how intuitive the system is to use.

- Check references: Become familiar with the supplier's clients. Ask what they implemented and why. Understand what other systems were evaluated and why they were not selected. Ask the tough questions about what went wrong, the pitfalls in the implementation process, and whether they got what they were promised, or minimally what they expected.

- Schedule customer visits: Get a firsthand look at how live end-users navigate throughout the system. See how programmers and project managers feel about the system. Ask detailed questions about the pains of implementation, the ease of upgrade installation, and migration and user acceptance.

- The above checklist items and plan will help get you the right selection.

Five Gigantic Mistakes Of E-Procurement

Mistake 1: Not creating a comprehensive procurement strategy first or a plan that aligns with an e-business strategy and e-procurement strategy.

The Institute of Supply Management notes that 95-percent of procurement organizations do not have a procurement strategy or long-term plan. Of the 5-percent that do have a strategy, only half have successfully aligned the strategy with overall business strategy. Most purchasing departments are continually embroiled in tactics and transactions. Much of their energy is diverted to the intensive transactions (80% of the work) and low-dollar-volume (20% of the dollars) aspects of the supply chain. E-procurement is a critical aspect of e-business, and must be incorporated into any e-business strategy.

Mistake 2: Putting the e- before procurement. Technology and e-procurement won't fix current unsound procurement practices.

A company must focus on its current business or procurement practices first. For many companies, these remain very archaic and transaction-intensive. The process of the reengineering of purchasing is an excellent first step in achieving the full benefits of e-procurement. This is where a comprehensive procurement assessment is mandatory. (The "as is" state). Standardized purchasing processes and rules are essential preceding steps. Procurement procedures should be clearly defined, along with current supplier-relationship depth. E-procurement is a powerful tool, but a disciplined procurement approach should be in place before e-procurement solutions are implemented. Again, the procurement must come before the e.

Mistake 3: Not performing strategic-supplier sourcing first and failing to prepare suppliers for e-procurement.

Strategic sourcing is a disciplined process organizations implement in order to more efficiently purchase goods and services from suppliers. The goal is to reduce total-acquisition cost while improving value. Forrester reports that 40-percent of the total reduction in costs is associated with technology while the other 60-percent is associated with strategic-sourcing techniques. Here are four key points to jump start strategic sourcing:

1. Understand the state of current spending.

2. Prepare a sourcing strategy for particular commodities, and tie the strategy into business and e-business strategy.

3. Evaluate the current competencies of your suppliers and how to extract value from these sources.

4. Decide what's important for you in your sourcing strategy and how it relates to selecting your technology solution.

Mistake 4: Not properly identifying materials-services groups and the proper e-procurement tool to use for these groups. Not assessing supplier capabilities, which include readiness for e-procurement. Initial step are:

The need to classify materials and services into particular categories is essential for the success of e-procurement. Each material group may require not only a different procurement strategy but also a different e-procurement solution. Companies often try to apply the same e-procurement strategy across the board to all materials and services. These categories demand different strategies, different types of suppliers, and different relationships, along with the use of different tools. Currently e-enabled tools do not exist for certain specific materials needs. They are, however, rapidly evolving.

The placement of a certain materials or services into a particular group may vary by company, industry, or a number of other factors. The key is to have and articulate a strategy by group and to utilize the appropriate tool.

Mistake 5: Underestimating resistance to change and the end-user's need for ease-of-use. A strong component in this area is content quality and the details of the transaction.

End-users demand ease of use and they want to quickly find the items that they need. Companies need to realise that e-procurement is competing with the easiest method to buy in the minds of their end-users. Many end-users would rather pick up a phone, tell their supplier what items they want, charge it to a corporate purchase card, and hang up. Unfortunately, in many companies, this method is still faster than using the current e-procurement software. Any impediments to the fast purchase of materials will quickly turn off end-users and kill transaction volumes. Speed is king in the world of e-procurement. End-users also want powerful search engines to quickly find their items. If the content of the supplier catalogue is poorly organized and the quality poor, end-users will quickly be frustrated by unfruitful searches and become non-users of the e-procurement system. In addition, special instructions that need to be given to suppliers about delivery or other issues can't easily be given with some e-procurement tools, or require additional end-user training, which raises the frustration levels.

Finally there is the relationship factor with new suppliers. Often new suppliers are installed for indirect materials solely because they seem to have more e-procurement capabilities. End-users value relationships with suppliers that they have trusted over the years. E-procurement is highly impersonal.

Resistance to change for an e-procurement system is fierce but can be readily overcome with strong commitment to change management. This change-management process must be an integral part of any e-procurement installation.

Never underestimate the role resistance to change plays in software implementation.

CHAPTER 16:
P-CARDS

Purchasing cards have been around from a long time. They still have many legitimate advantages for the supply management professional. This chapter provides some general guidelines and thoughts on purchase cards.

How To Sell Procurement Cards

Procurement cards are still a proven best practice. Card providers are constantly upgrading their systems, reports, and software, and continuously improving the functionality of the cards. So why are so many purchasing departments unable to implement a procurement-card program? There are many reasons, including the fact that implementing procurement cards can demand an outstanding internal sales program and intense persuasion of your internal customers. If this is the case in your organization, brush up on your sales skills. One of the biggest barriers to implementing a procurement-card program is selling the concept internally. Such a crucial sell requires excellent sales and marketing skills. The good news is that these skills can be learned. Here are some guidelines to help you sell the procurement-card program.

Procurement Card Pre-Work Tips:

- Target your savings. Get a good projection on the number of transactions that will be eliminated and exactly what items can be purchased with the cards. Get the hard savings calculated right first, including reductions in mailing, checks, time, and forms.

- Establish in advance which suppliers will accept the procurement card. This will help eliminate initial teething pains with inexperienced suppliers.

- Establish a transaction cost and include it in your savings. Many accounting and consulting firms can calculate this cost for you and boost the credibility of your savings.

- Involve as many parties as possible in the pre-work stage, especially accounting and receiving. If possible, conduct site visits to firms that have successfully implemented procurement-card programs, and arrange face-to-face meetings with the accounting and receiving departments to help your internal people understand the concept, learn from their experiences, and alleviate their fears.

Purchase Cards—The Two Biggest Fears

The two biggest fears that you need to deal with are control and security fraud. During your "sales" presentation, make sure that you present all the safeguards against fraud. Control is one of the strongest selling points of procurement cards. Contrast the elaborate controls available with procurement cards as compared to your current small-purchase control system. If you do not address and eliminate these two fears from every angle possible, you will not sell the procurement-card program. Enlist a champion, preferably at the vice president or director level, to understand the procurement-card program and assist you in its implementation.

Target Key Groups For Purchase Cards

Target your controller and key accountants for even more persuasion. Listen carefully to their concerns and address them. Constant reassurance of the "best-practice nature" concept of the procurement card can be accomplished via some pre-sell methods such as meetings with key requisitioners, alliances with maintenance personnel (who usually become the procurement card's strongest proponents), and finding out if your competitors are using procurement cards. Ask your suppliers if they are willing to give personal testimonials about procurement cards and how the transaction data is gathered at their site.

Fine-Tune The Purchase-Card Presentation

Limit your presentation to no more than thirty minutes. Be specific about your rollout plan, objectives, goals, savings, and impact on other departments. Be prepared to answer the tough questions about control and security fraud. The procurement-card concept is a strategic tool that can help purchasing professionals escape the paperwork swamp. Preparation and marketing are essential for procurement-card acceptance in your organization. Concentrate your resources in these two areas, and your sales presentation should be well received.

Some More Tips For Purchasing Cards

Credit-card purchases by end-users (your internal customers) can be one of the Win-Win results of transformation purchasing. With these direct purchases, end-users are empowered to purchase routine or necessary items. Many purchasing departments clearly see these tremendous transaction-cost savings but aren't sure how to train end-users to purchase directly with procurement cards or via other methods. The simplest and most effective way to implement this empowerment is to publish a purchasing-information manual designed just for them.

Develop A Purchase Card Manual

The manual's primary purpose should be to give down-to-earth "nuts and bolts" instructions. Give clear pointers with concrete examples. Make sure card users receive some basic ethical ground rules and a written company policy on gifts and gratuities, and help them get familiar with rudimentary contract law. Make sure you have the entire purchasing department contribute to the manual. Other key internal departments such as accounting, accounts payable, and receiving can also provide valuable input to further streamline the transaction cycle.

Contents Of The Purchase-Card Manual

Try to keep the manual brief and to the point. Limit the number of pages. Three-ring binders provide the option of quickly adding and removing information in the future. Open the manual with a table of contents and divide it into sections via labeled tabs or dividers. The manual should include a purchasing organizational chart and the specific responsibilities of purchasers. Provide a glossary of typical purchasing terms and some basic purchasing policies and goals, along with emergency contacts. Have a section where purchasing newsletters or flyers can be accumulated, and insert a feedback form in each manual that can be sent to purchasing with end-user suggestions.

More Details About Purchase Cards

Encourage end-users to use procurement cards first whenever possible. Draw analogies to using a personal credit card. List the names and telephone numbers of in-house administrators, along with the 1-800 telephone help numbers of your purchase-card provider. Provide examples of internal control forms and a list of preferred suppliers who accept the cards. Give specific examples of what to do when items are to be returned or a charge is disputed. Pre-qualify suppliers by having purchasing perform at least one purchase via the corporate purchasing card and review all the subsequent reports.

P-Card Rollout Tips

If possible; publicize the manual's rollout in your purchasing or company newsletter. Have a formal kick-off meeting with the entire purchasing team present. Give out the manual at training sessions. Provide smaller training classes for the key end-users so questions can be answered before the manual is used. Inform your key preferred suppliers about the manual, and give them copies if they desire. Prepare suppliers for the end-user procurement card purchases, alerting them that questions may arise from the end-users. All the manuals should be numbered, and an issue-log kept so that you know who has been issued a copy. A master copy should be kept in a safe place with pending updates and revisions nearby.

Follow-Up To The Purchase-Card Manual

Every member of the purchasing department should have a copy of the manual. When internal customers arrive in the department with questions, purchasing department members should sit down with them and guide them to the answers in the manual. A purchasing-information manual is one aspect of training employees companywide for procurement-card use.

Some Pitfalls For Purchase Cards

Just about any supplier or business will accept them. Some employees will abuse them. Be prepared to deal with them immediately. Purchase-card transaction information is often vague or incomplete. My best advice is to limit or only use them with a group of preferred, trusted suppliers.

CHAPTER 17:
THE PERILS OF GLOBAL SOURCING

Global sourcing is a complicated process with even more variables than typical supplier sourcing. The methodology of sourcing remains the same, but there are many more variables added that have to be considered. I have often used a broker or representative to help handle these complexities when dealing with another country and have found that this method has been the most successful for me, my company, and the particular item being sourced. Yes, there can be an extra cost with using a broker, but I have found that the benefits far outweigh the costs. However, there are international, federal, and state trade resources very available to help.

Some Reasons To Source Globally

There are many reasons to source globally, and the most prevalent is reducing costs. Other factors may include expanding your market, optimizing the supply chain, and expanding your global presence. Obtaining internal high-level support is crucial for any global-sourcing decision.

The Complexities Of Global Sourcing

It's impossible to cover all the differences and complexities for every country in this book. Some of them include currency issues, political stability, infrastructure issues, contract-law differences, high logistics costs, protectionism, and lack of managerial talent. However, there are methodologies available to help you at least have a checklist for such a global-sourcing challenge. Make sure you do a current "as-is" of your supply chain and a future "to-be." It's critical to develop delivered or all in costs.

Why Culture Can Make Or Break The Process

If you decide to deal directly with the source or supplier in another country, you need to realize that reaching a strong cultural understanding will make or break the process. The task of understanding the culture of the sourcing country is the most difficult of the entire process. Culture includes social organization, political beliefs, the legal system, religious beliefs, language, and the educational system, to name just a few. Any one of these areas requires extensive study and understanding in order to be successful. It is no small task.

Site Visits Are Even More Important; Trace The Supply Chain

Site visits are even more important with a global supplier along with frequent inspections of the product or service. I once jokingly said that we should trace the supply chain in person, following our product from the foreign plant through the entire logistics chain and then process-map it. We actually did this, having a person ride the ship across the Pacific Ocean! Never underestimate what can go wrong during the logistics portion of the supply chain.

Fundamental Lean Six Sigma And Supply Management Glossary Of Terms

Analyze
Analyze is a DMAIC phase where process detail and data are scrutinized for improvement opportunities.

Best Practices
A method that is proven superior to other methods.

Black Belt
Black Belts are Six Sigma project-team leaders, who become expert in the use of the Lean Six Sigma methodologies and tools. A key responsibility of Black Belts is to share their knowledge and to train others. Black Belts are normally devoted to business-improvement activities fulltime.

Brainstorming
A technique used by teams to generate ideas on a particular subject or to explore a particular problem. Each individual involved is asked to think creatively about the issue, and write down as many ideas as possible. Following this, each point raised is discussed in more detail.

Buckets
A market basket of similar or related products.

Business Case

A *business case* is a structured proposal for business process improvement that functions as a decision package for enterprise leadership. A business case includes an analysis of business process needs or problems, proposed solution, assumptions and constraints, alternatives, life cycle costs, benefits/cost analysis, and investment risk analysis.

Charter

A written commitment between a Six Sigma team and the organization, the *charter* includes the business case, problem and goal statements, constraints and assumptions, roles, preliminary plans, scope, and the roles of participants in the project. This document states the scope of authority for an improvement project or team, and is approved by management. Periodic reviews with the sponsor ensure alignment with business strategies. Charters should be reviewed, revised, and refined periodically throughout the DMAIC process, based on data.

Company culture

This is a system of values, beliefs, and behaviors inherent in a company. The *company culture* has a strong effect on business performance, so top management needs to define and create the correct culture in order to ensure optimum performance.

Control

The *Control* phase is DMAIC Phase C. Once solutions have been implemented, ongoing measures track and verify the stability of the improvement and the predictability of the process. This stage often includes process-management techniques and systems including process ownership, cockpit charts, and/or process-management charts.

Customer

A *customer* is the person, place, or thing for which a particular process adds value. *Customers* can be grouped as *internal customers* and *external customers* (paying).

Cycle Time

Cycle time is the total time from the beginning to the end of your process, as defined by you and your customer.

Data

Data is any fact used as a basis for reasoning, discussion, or calculation; often this term refers to quantitative information. There are two basic classifications of numerical data:

1) Measured, variable, or continuous data

2) Attribute or counted data.

Defect

Any result that does not conform to the standard needed to satisfy the customer's requirements. The propensity to generate *defects* increases as process capability is lost, which in turn increases process variation. The creation of *defects* results in extra cost, delay, inventory, debtors, loss of capacity, stress and frustration, as well as in damaging customer relationships.

Define

Define is the first DMAIC phase. It defines the problem/opportunity, process, and customer requirements. Because the DMAIC cycle is iterative, the process, problem, flow, and requirements should be verified and updated for clarity throughout the other phases.

Deployment

This is the dispersion, dissemination, broadcasting, or spreading of a communication downward and laterally throughout an organization. It also describes the putting into action of a strategy, improvement plan, or process.

Deployment Champion (also known as Deployment Director)

A senior-level manager, normally reporting to an Executive Team, who is responsible for the successful management of the deployment plan, coordinates Lean Six Sigma policy, planning, and execution. Generally an organization will have a fulltime *Deployment Champion* if they have fifteen or more Black Belts assigned.

DMAIC

Define, Measure, Analyze, Improve, and Control. These are the steps of a Lean Six Sigma project. Define the real problem to be solved; collect data that defines the issues; analyze the data using statistical techniques; develop an improvement based on the analysis; put the improvement in place and control it, so that it continues to provide benefit over time.

ERP

Enterprise resource planning systems integrate internal and external management information across an entire organization. The purpose is to integrate information to improve performance.

Evergreen Contract

A contract between two parties that is automatically renewed.

First Time Through

This is the idea that quality is achieved at its lowest cost by producing your product or service right the first time, without rework.

Five Whys

This is a simple problem solving method of analyzing a problem or issue by asking *"Why?"* five times. The root cause should become evident by continuing to ask *why* a situation exists.

Flow Chart

This is a visible problem-solving tool that illustrates a process. It can show the "as-is" process or "should-be" process for comparison and should make waste evident.

Goal Statement

A *goal statement* is a description of the intended target or desired results of Process-Improvement or Design/Redesign activities. It's usually included in a team charter and supported with actual numbers and details once data has been obtained.

Green Belt

A *Green Belt* is a team member who demonstrates an interest in, and aptitude for, the Lean Six Sigma methodologies and tools. They receive basic training in the techniques, which they use either in support of a Black Belt project, or to run their own projects typically in their own area of responsibility. *Green Belts* are normally assigned part time to Six Sigma project activities, although in most cases, they use Six Sigma methods as part of their normal jobs.

Green Initiatives
Environmentally friendly initiatives or projects.

Hypothesis Testing
The application of statistical tests to a data sample, in order to determine what cannot be concluded based on the data (the results of hypothesis testing are either a rejection of the hypothesis or a failure to reject). *Hypothesis testing* can be conducted with attribute and continuous data and on normal and non-normal samples. The tests will be different based on the nature of the data.

Hidden Factory
This is a concept for showing the costs of creating quality without using Lean or Six Sigma. In the *hidden factory,* there are a number of stations where rework or scrap is created, in order to achieve a quality target. The goal of Lean Six Sigma is to remove the requirement for rework and scrap while increasing quality. The result is higher quality at a lower cost.

Hoshin Kanri
This is a strategy that literally means "to move the whole ship in the right direction." It refers to the requirement that all improvement projects meet the strategic needs of the organization.

Improve
Improve is a DMAIC phase where solutions and ideas are creatively generated and decided upon. Once a problem has been fully identified, measured, and analyzed, potential solutions can be determined to solve the problem in the problem statement and support the goal statement.

Just in Time

Just in time is a Lean concept that aims to deliver products and services to the customer only as they are requested. It goes beyond the pull-systems concept, in that it addresses the timing of the process and process communications. It answers questions such as, "When must I start this process step in order to have a product ready for the customer when they ask for it?"

Kaizen

Kaizen is a term meaning "continuous improvement." In Lean Six Sigma terms, it refers to a project performed at the work-group level that will remove waste from a process. These types of projects can be performed quickly (usually in less than two months).

Lean Six Sigma

Lean Six Sigma is a method by which processes are improved for quality; cost; speed and accuracy. It is the combination of Lean Methods and Six Sigma.

Lead Time

Lead time is the amount of time, defined by the supplier, which is required to meet a customer request or demand. (Note that *lead time* is not the same as *cycle time.)*

Lean Methods

A set of tools designed to improve a process on a continuous basis. *Lean* is designed to remove waste from a process by identifying non-value-added steps. Lean will improve process speed to conform to customer requirements. With *Lean,* we say that *waste is the enemy.* It was developed by Taichi Ohno at the Toyota Motor Company from the 1950s to the 1980s.

Lean Six Sigma

This is a business-improvement methodology that maximizes shareholder value by achieving the fastest rate of improvement in customer satisfaction, cost, quality, process speed, and invested capital.

Master Black Belt

Master Black Belts are Six Sigma quality experts that are responsible for the strategic implementations within an organization. *Master Black Belts'* main responsibilities include training and mentoring of Black Belts and Green Belts; helping to prioritize, select and charter high-impact projects, maintaining the integrity of the Six Sigma measurements, improvements, and tollgates; and developing, maintaining, and revising Six Sigma training materials.

The *Master Black Belt* should be qualified to teach other Six Sigma facilitators the methodologies, tools, and applications in all functions and levels of the company, and should be a resource for using statistical-process control (typically just outside the Black Belt's knowledge base) within processes.

Measure

DMAIC phase M, where key measures are identified, and data are collected, compiled, and displayed.

Metrics, Process (or Input)

Metrics are the subset of measures, the improvement of which have a direct positive effect on results *metrics*.

Metrics, Results

This is the subset of measures, the improvement of which is critical to the success of the organization. A change in *results met-*

rics will directly and significantly affect customer or stakeholder satisfaction.

Non-Value-Added (NVA)
Any product, process, or service that does not add value to the customer.

Output
The *output* is the result of a process. Usually it corresponds to the deliverables of the process, such as products, services, processes, plans, and resources.

Policy
Policy is a direction plan for achieving an organization's goals.

Poke-Yoke
Poke-yoke is a term that means error-proof. Error-proofing is one of the holy grails of Lean Six Sigma projects. It means that because of the process improvement, it is now impossible for an error to occur. Examples are computer fields that automatically fill in based on other information entered, or an email that is automatically sent when an event occurs.

Preferred Supplier Status
A supplier that has been approved by the customer for purchase of products or services.

Process
A *process* is a series of steps and interrelated work activities, characterized by specific inputs, and tasks which add value, and make up a procedure for a set of specific outputs.

Process Map

A *process map* is a type of flow chart that provides an illustrated description of how things get done. It enables participants to visualize an entire process and identify areas of strength and weakness. It helps reduce cycle time and defects while recognizing the value of individual contributions.

Process Owner

A *process owner* is the individual(s) responsible for process design and performance. The *process owner* is accountable for sustaining the gain and identifying future improvement opportunities for the process.

Project Scoping

The general term used for the process of developing project ideas. A well-*scoped* project will have the following characteristics:

- It can be completed within 4–6 months.

- It will solve a defect that is within the commands' span of control.

- It will deal with a process that repeats itself quite often.

- The defect it addresses is measurable, and the possibility to collect data exists.

- It will result in an improvement that is important to the customers of the process.

- It will result in a 50% process improvement or $250,000 savings.

Project Sponsor (also known as Project Champion)

A *project sponsor* is the senior/middle-level manager responsible for the selection and support of black and green belts, and with the selection and management of Six Sigma improvement projects.

Project Team

A *project team* is the team managing the work and activities of a project. The work typically involves balancing competing demands for project scope, time, cost, risk, and quality, satisfying stakeholders with differing needs and expectations and meeting identified requirements.

Pull Systems

A *pull system* is a process that only responds to customer demand. The idea is that work done that is not in response to customer demand is wasted effort.

Root Cause

A *root cause* is an identified reason for the presence of a defect or problem. The most basic reason, which if eliminated, would prevent recurrence. A root cause is the source or origin of an event.

Sample

A *sample* is a portion of the whole collection of items (population).

SIPOC

SIPOC stands for **s**uppliers, **i**nputs, **p**rocess, **o**utputs, and **c**ustomers and form the columns of a table.

Six Sigma

This is a term used to describe a system of process improvement. The goal of *Six Sigma* is to identify customer requirements, reduce variation of a process that is targeted by that requirement, and center the process results on the customer target. In *Six Sigma,* we say, *Variation is the enemy.* It was invented by Mikel Harry in the early 1980s at Motorola.

Spend Data

The information and data on what an organization spends its money on.

Stakeholder

Stakeholders are people affected by the project or who can influence it but who are not directly involved with doing the project work. Examples are managers affected by the project, process owners, people who work with the process under study, internal departments that support the process, customers, suppliers, and the financial department.

Strategic Sourcing

A process that continually improves, evaluates and sources the products and services that an organization needs.

Takt Time

Takt time is the pace of customer demand. If a customer demands eight products per eight-hour day, then the takt time is one hour. You must have the capacity to produce one product every hour in order to meet customer demand.

Time to Market

The time that it takes for a product to be conceived until actual sale.

Tollgate Review
This is the component of DMAIC that helps to ensure that the project requirements of a phase are met before starting the next one. At the end of each phase, Black Belts and team members meet to review that the requirements of the DMAIC phase have been completed. It is an excellent communication tool for keeping the team involved in the process.

Total Cost of Ownership
All the direct and indirect costs of a product, service or system.

Train the trainer
A training process that usually takes a corporate employee and trains them to be a professional trainer.

Upper and Lower Statistical Limits
These are the limits that define quality. They are set by the customer. If a customer demands that deliveries be made within two to four days, then those are your LSL and USL. Any delivery that falls outside those limits is a defect.

Value Added
Activities or work essential to ensure a product or service meets the needs of the customer.

Value-Stream Mapping
Value-stream mapping is a method of visualizing a process so that improvements can be made to it. It includes process steps, methods for communicating requirements to each process step, and data that describes each process step. VSM is an important starting point for most DMAIC projects. There are three processes associated with VSM: the current state (what you think the

process is), the current state (what the process really is), and the future state.

Visual Factory

All Lean improvement rests on the idea that everything should be visible, so that if there is a problem someone will notice and take action. The *visual factory* has six levels:

1) Share information

2) Share standards at the site

3) Build standards into the workplace

4) Warn about abnormalities

5) Stop abnormalities, and

6) Prevent abnormalities.

Voice of the Customer (VOC)

VOC is the customer-feedback system. It may consist of meetings, surveys, or interviews that gather customer feedback in a form that may be acted upon. Since the majority of improvements are designed to improve customer service, this is critical.

Waste

Any activity or product that consumes resources and produces no added value to the product or service a customer receives.

What if Scenarios

Analysis of different situations and the different results.

Work in Process

Unfinished production materials that are not yet ready for sale.

Y=f(X)

Refers to cause and effect and is a tool for root-cause analysis. An output variable Y is dependent on the inputs of one or more independent variables X. Lean Six Sigma projects focus on improving Y, through the improvement of a "key" X variable. That means we should be treating causes, not symptoms. $Y=f(X)$ analysis is used as a brainstorming tool for identifying project opportunities and as a tool to ensure that the project is properly focused.

Zero Out

Reduce an item or inventory to nothing or zero.

You can contact the author at www.commonsensesupply management.com

INDEX

T

Made in the USA
Columbia, SC
30 March 2022

58319921R00111